Mastering Motorola Razr 2024 Flip Features and Functions

Essential Guide to Setup Customization and Advanced Tips

Elara Technova

i

COPYRIGHT

This non-fiction book is based on the authors thorough research and personal experiences. Despite diligent efforts to ensure accuracy and completeness in the information presented, neither the author nor the publisher can be held liable for any mistakes, oversights, or consequences arising from the use of the information contained within.

※ Elara Technova

Disclaimer

This guide is an independent publication and is not affiliated with or endorsed by the manufacturer of the product. All trademarks and product names are the property of their respective owners. While every effort has been made to ensure accuracy, the author and publisher are not liable for any errors, omissions, or outcomes resulting from the use of this guide. For official support, refer to the product manufacturer.

※ Elara Technova

About the Author

Elara Technova is a trusted authority in technology writing, known for her remarkable ability to make complex concepts clear and approachable. With a strong background in Computer Science, she masterfully transforms intricate technical details into practical, step-by-step guides. Her work empowers readers of all skill levels to confidently understand and use the latest technology, making it accessible for everyone in today's rapidly advancing digital world.

✻ Elara Technova

Contents

Introduction

The Motorola Razr 2024 Flip represents a significant step forward in foldable smartphone technology. By blending the iconic design of the classic Razr with modern features and performance capabilities, this device stands out in a competitive market. This chapter provides a comprehensive overview of the evolution of the Motorola Razr series, the key features of the 2024 Flip model, the audience this guide caters to,

1

and an outline of the essential topics covered in the book.

Evolution of Motorola Razr Series

The Motorola Razr is one of the most iconic names in mobile phone history. Originally launched in 2004, the Razr V3 became a cultural phenomenon, celebrated for its slim design, unique clamshell form, and futuristic appeal. This device redefined the concept of mobile design during a time when most phones were bulky and functional but lacked style.

Fast forward to the modern era, Motorola breathed new life into the Razr brand with the introduction of foldable smartphones. The first modern Razr, launched in 2019, combined nostalgia with innovation, bringing back the clamshell design but replacing the traditional keypad with a fully functional touchscreen. It featured a foldable OLED display that folded seamlessly into the compact form factor users adored.

Over the years, Motorola refined the Razr lineup with incremental improvements in hardware, display technology, software, and overall durability. The Motorola Razr 2024 Flip is the culmination of this evolution. It addresses previous limitations while introducing cutting-edge features such as improved foldable screen technology, enhanced battery life, and advanced camera systems. This model reflects Motorola's dedication to innovation and its desire to blend style with substance, making it an essential choice for those who value both aesthetics and performance in their devices.

Key Features of the Razr 2024 Flip

The Motorola Razr 2024 Flip is packed with features designed to meet the needs of modern smartphone users while staying true to its heritage of stylish design. Here are the standout features of this remarkable device:

- **Foldable pOLED Display Technology**: The main display is a stunning 6.9-inch Full HD+ pOLED screen with a crisp 2640 x 1080 resolution. Its vibrant colors and sharp clarity make it ideal for everything from watching videos to reading documents. The external 3.6-inch cover display is equally impressive, allowing users to check notifications, control music, or even capture selfies without opening the phone.
- **Compact and Durable Design**: Despite its foldable nature, the Razr 2024 Flip is built to last. It features Corning® Gorilla® Glass Victus on the outer surfaces, a vegan leather back for a premium feel, and a sturdy

aluminum frame. The IPX8 water resistance ensures protection against splashes and brief submersion.

- **High-Performance Hardware**: Powered by the MediaTek Dimensity 7300 chipset, the Razr 2024 Flip ensures smooth performance across applications, gaming, and multitasking. The 8GB RAM and 256GB internal storage provide ample space for media and apps, while the 4200mAh battery supports both 30W TurboPower™ fast charging and 15W wireless charging.
- **Advanced Camera System**: The dual-camera setup includes a 50MP main sensor with Optical Image Stabilization for clear and vibrant shots and a 13MP ultra-wide/macro camera for capturing diverse perspectives. A 32MP front-facing camera ensures high-quality selfies and video calls.
- **Enhanced Connectivity**: With 5G compatibility, Wi-Fi 6/6E, Bluetooth 5.4, and NFC, the Razr 2024 Flip ensures fast and reliable connections for streaming, gaming, and payments.
- **User-Friendly Software**: Running on Android 14, the Razr 2024 Flip offers a clean and intuitive user experience. It integrates seamlessly with Google apps and

services while offering customization options to suit individual preferences.

These features make the Motorola Razr 2024 Flip a versatile and powerful device suitable for a wide range of users, from productivity enthusiasts to content creators and casual users.

Who This Guide is For

This guide is designed to help anyone who owns or is considering purchasing the Motorola Razr 2024 Flip. It caters to a diverse audience, including:

- **New Users**: If you've just bought the Razr 2024 Flip and feel overwhelmed by its features, this guide will walk you through the setup process and introduce you to its functionalities in a simple and straightforward way.
- **Tech Enthusiasts**: For those who enjoy exploring the latest gadgets and pushing them to their limits, this guide delves into advanced settings, customization options, and hidden features.
- **Professionals and Students**: Whether you need the Razr for work or studies, this guide provides tips on productivity tools, multitasking features, and integrating the device into your daily routine.

- **Foldable Technology Fans**: If you're intrigued by foldable smartphones and want to make the most of this innovative form factor, this guide will show you how to maximize its unique capabilities.

No matter your level of experience or your reasons for using the Razr 2024 Flip, this guide ensures you'll unlock the full potential of your device with ease.

Overview of What You'll Learn

This book covers every aspect of the Motorola Razr 2024 Flip, ensuring you have the knowledge and skills to use it confidently. Here's a snapshot of what you'll learn:

- **Setup and Configuration**: Learn how to unbox, set up, and customize your device for optimal performance.
- **Optimizing Performance**: Explore tips for enhancing battery life, improving connectivity, and speeding up your device.
- **Camera Mastery**: Get the most out of the Razr's advanced camera features, from taking professional-quality photos to recording cinematic videos.

- **Customization and Personalization**: Discover how to make the Razr truly yours by adjusting themes, layouts, and shortcuts.
- **Advanced Features**: Dive into the foldable display technology, multitasking options, and gaming settings that set the Razr apart.
- **Maintenance and Troubleshooting**: Learn how to keep your Razr running smoothly and solve common problems effectively.

With this guide in hand, you'll not only master the basics but also uncover the advanced features that make the Motorola Razr 2024 Flip a truly unique device. This book ensures you'll maximize your investment, enjoy your phone to the fullest, and stay ahead in the ever-evolving world of smartphones.

Unboxing and Initial Setup

Getting started with your Motorola Razr 2024 Flip is an exciting experience. The design, technology, and features of this foldable phone are a testament to Motorola's innovation. This chapter is dedicated to guiding you through the unboxing process, setting up the device for the first time, installing essential apps, and addressing common setup issues to ensure your journey begins smoothly.

Unboxing your Motorola Razr 2024 Flip is the first step toward exploring its features and capabilities. The packaging is thoughtfully designed to protect the device and accessories during transit. Inside the box, you'll find the Motorola Razr 2024 Flip wrapped in protective film, highlighting its sleek foldable design. Alongside the phone, there's a 30W TurboPower™ charger to ensure quick charging, a USB-C cable for charging and data transfer, a SIM ejector tool for inserting or removing the SIM card, a quick start guide to provide an overview of setup steps, and warranty information detailing the terms and conditions of product support.

Carefully remove all items from the box and inspect them for any signs of damage. If you notice anything unusual, such as scratches on the device or missing components, contact Motorola's support team or the retailer where you purchased the phone. Once confirmed that everything is in order, peel off the protective film from the device, revealing its premium finish and foldable display. Handle the phone gently during this process to avoid accidental drops or fingerprints on the screen.

Setting up your Motorola Razr 2024 Flip for the first time is an essential step that prepares the device for use. Begin by powering on the device by pressing and holding the power button located on the side of the phone. The Motorola logo will appear, signaling that the device is booting up. Once the phone is on, the screen will prompt you to select your preferred language. Tap on the language you're comfortable with, then proceed to the next step.

The next step involves inserting your SIM card. Use the SIM ejector tool included in the box to open the SIM tray. Carefully place your SIM card in the tray, ensuring it aligns with the cutout, and gently slide the tray back into the phone. If you plan to use an eSIM, follow the on-screen instructions to activate it. After setting up the SIM, connect to a Wi-Fi network by selecting your network name from the list and entering the password. A stable internet connection is crucial at this stage, as the phone may download software updates and synchronize with cloud services.

You'll then be prompted to sign in to your Google account. Enter your credentials to access Google services like Gmail, Google Drive, and the Play Store. If you don't have a Google account, you can create one during this step. After signing in, the setup process will guide you to configure biometric security options, including fingerprint recognition and face unlock. These features enhance your device's security while making it convenient to unlock.

The setup wizard also includes an option to transfer data from your previous device. If you wish to migrate your contacts, photos, and apps, use the device's built-in transfer tool or follow the steps to connect your old phone. The final step involves customizing basic settings, such as enabling dark mode, adjusting display brightness, and setting notification preferences. Once complete, the phone is ready for use.

Installing Essential Apps

With the device set up, the next step is to install apps that cater to your needs and lifestyle. The Motorola Razr 2024 Flip, running on Android 14, provides access to the Google Play Store, where millions of apps are available for download. Start by installing communication apps like WhatsApp, Telegram, and Zoom to stay in touch with family, friends, and colleagues. For productivity, consider apps like Google Drive, Microsoft Office, and Evernote, which help manage work and personal tasks efficiently.

If you enjoy social media, download Instagram, Facebook, TikTok, or Twitter to stay connected with the latest trends and share your moments. For entertainment, streaming apps like Netflix, Disney+, YouTube, and Spotify are perfect for enjoying movies, shows, and music. If fitness is a priority, apps like MyFitnessPal, Google Fit, or Strava can help you track your health and workouts. Additionally, install banking and financial apps to manage your accounts and transactions securely.

After downloading these apps, organize them into folders or arrange them on your home screen for quick access. For example, create a "Work" folder for productivity apps and a "Social" folder for social media platforms. This keeps your home screen clutter-free and makes navigation easier.

Common Setup Issues and Solutions

While setting up your Motorola Razr 2024 Flip, you may encounter some challenges. Knowing how to address these issues can save time and prevent frustration.

One common issue is difficulty connecting to Wi-Fi. Ensure that your Wi-Fi router is functioning properly and is within range of the device. If you're unable to connect, restart both your router and phone. Double-check the Wi-Fi password for accuracy. If problems persist, consider forgetting the network and reconnecting.

Another issue users face is trouble signing in to a Google account. Verify that your email address and password are correct. If you've forgotten your password, use the "Forgot Password" option to reset it. Ensure your internet connection is stable, as this can affect the sign-in process.

Sometimes, the SIM card may not be detected. Check that the SIM is inserted correctly in the tray. If the problem continues, try inserting the SIM into another phone to confirm its functionality. If the SIM works in another device, contact Motorola's support team for further assistance.

Biometric setup issues, such as fingerprint recognition not working, can be resolved by cleaning the fingerprint sensor and ensuring your hands are dry. If the problem persists, re-register your fingerprint. For face unlock, ensure that you're in a well-lit area and that the camera lens is clean.

If the device is slow during setup due to initial updates, be patient and ensure it remains connected to a stable Wi-Fi network. Avoid interrupting the update process, as this could cause errors. For app installation errors, clear the Play Store cache and restart the device before trying again.

By addressing these common issues proactively, you can ensure a smooth setup experience and begin enjoying your Motorola Razr 2024 Flip without unnecessary delays. This chapter equips you with the knowledge to confidently unbox, set up, and prepare your device for daily use, setting the stage for an exceptional smartphone experience.

Getting to Know Your Razr 2024 Flip

The Motorola Razr 2024 Flip combines a sleek foldable design with advanced technology to offer an innovative smartphone experience. Understanding its unique features and layout is essential to make the most of this device. This chapter provides a detailed explanation of the foldable design, the main and external display features, the physical layout and buttons, and practical tips for first-time users. By the end of this chapter, you will feel confident in navigating and using your Razr 2024 Flip efficiently.

Exploring the Foldable Design

The Motorola Razr 2024 Flip's foldable design is its most defining feature, blending nostalgia with modern innovation. The phone folds compactly into a pocket-friendly size, making it easy to carry and handle. When unfolded, it reveals a 6.9-inch pOLED display that offers stunning visuals with vibrant colors and deep contrasts. This foldable display technology not only adds a wow factor but also enhances the usability of the device by combining portability with a large screen experience.

The hinge mechanism is engineered for durability, ensuring a smooth folding and unfolding experience. Motorola has designed this hinge to minimize creases on the screen, a common challenge in foldable smartphones. The hinge allows for flexible use cases, such as propping the phone partially open to watch videos hands-free, participate in video calls, or take group selfies. This "Flex View" mode expands how you can interact with your phone.

To ensure the longevity of the foldable design, Motorola has incorporated materials like Corning® Gorilla® Glass Victus on the outer shell and high-strength aluminum in the frame. Additionally, the phone is IPX8-rated for water resistance, offering protection against splashes and accidental submersion in water. These design elements make the Razr 2024 Flip both stylish and robust, suitable for everyday use.

Main and External Display Features

The Motorola Razr 2024 Flip features two displays: a 6.9-inch Full HD+ pOLED main display and a 3.6-inch external pOLED cover screen. Both screens are integral to the device's functionality and user experience.

The **main display** is the centerpiece of the Razr 2024 Flip. With a resolution of 2640 x 1080 pixels, it delivers sharp and vibrant visuals, making it ideal for watching videos, browsing the web, or playing games. The screen supports HDR10+ for enhanced contrast and color accuracy, ensuring an immersive viewing experience. Its 144Hz refresh rate ensures smooth scrolling and fluid animations, especially useful for gaming and high-speed content.

The **external display**, on the other hand, provides quick access to essential features without unfolding the phone. With a resolution of 1056 x 1066 pixels, it is perfect for checking notifications, controlling music, and using widgets. The cover screen supports various customizations, allowing you to personalize widgets like weather updates, calendar events, or quick shortcuts to frequently used apps.

One standout feature of the external display is its ability to serve as a viewfinder for the rear camera. This allows you to take high-quality selfies using the powerful dual-camera system, offering better detail and clarity compared to the front-facing camera. The external screen also supports touch gestures for quick navigation, such as swiping to dismiss notifications or tapping to open apps.

Understanding the Layout and Buttons

The physical layout of the Motorola Razr 2024 Flip is thoughtfully designed for ease of use and functionality. Familiarizing yourself with its buttons and ports will help you navigate the device effortlessly.

- **Power Button**: Located on the right-hand side of the device, the power button doubles as a fingerprint sensor. This placement ensures quick and secure unlocking while being ergonomically convenient.

- **Volume Rocker**: Positioned above the power button, the volume rocker allows you to adjust sound levels for calls, media, and alarms.
- **SIM Tray**: Found on the left-hand side, the SIM tray can be accessed using the SIM ejector tool included in the box. It supports either a physical SIM card or an eSIM configuration.
- **USB-C Port**: Located at the bottom of the phone, the USB-C port is used for charging and data transfer.
- **Speakers and Microphones**: The phone features stereo speakers and multiple microphones, ensuring clear audio for calls, recordings, and media playback.

The Razr's foldable design includes a seamless hinge mechanism at its center, which allows the phone to fold and unfold smoothly. The top and bottom edges are rounded for a comfortable grip, while the overall design ensures the phone is easy to operate with one or both hands.

Essential Tips for First-Time Users

Getting started with the Motorola Razr 2024 Flip can feel overwhelming, especially if it's your first foldable phone. Here are some essential tips to help you navigate and maximize your experience with the device:

- **Use the External Display Efficiently**: The cover screen is designed for quick interactions. Customize it with widgets like weather, music controls, or fitness stats for convenient access to information at a glance. You can also set up shortcuts to your most-used apps, reducing the need to unfold the phone constantly.
- **Protect the Foldable Screen**: The main display is designed for durability but requires some care. Avoid pressing too hard on the screen, and use the protective case provided by Motorola or a third-party option to safeguard the device.
- **Enable Flex View Mode**: Experiment with the phone's ability to stay partially open in Flex View mode. This feature is particularly useful for video calls, watching videos, or taking photos without a tripod.
- **Explore Display Settings**: Adjust the main display settings to suit your preferences. Enable dark mode to reduce eye strain and save battery life. Customize the refresh rate to balance performance and power efficiency.

- **Master the Gestures**: The Motorola Razr 2024 Flip supports intuitive gestures for navigation. For example, you can swipe up from the bottom to return to the home screen, swipe from the side to go back, and swipe up and hold to access recent apps.
- **Optimize Battery Usage**: To extend battery life, enable the phone's battery saver mode and lower the brightness of the external display. Additionally, close unused apps running in the background.
- **Take Advantage of Quick Capture**: Use the double-twist gesture to quickly launch the camera app, allowing you to capture moments instantly without navigating through menus.
- **Explore Preinstalled Apps**: Motorola includes several helpful apps tailored for the Razr, such as Moto Actions and Moto Display. These apps provide additional functionality, such as quick gestures and personalized notifications.

By understanding the foldable design, leveraging both displays, and becoming familiar with the phone's layout and features, first-time users can seamlessly integrate the Motorola Razr 2024 Flip into their daily lives. This knowledge will not only enhance the usability of the device but also allow you to appreciate its innovative design and functionality.

Android 14 Operating System

The Motorola Razr 2024 Flip runs on Android 14, Google's latest operating system, offering a seamless, user-friendly experience with enhanced features, customization options, and robust security measures. This chapter provides a comprehensive understanding of Android 14 and how it integrates with the Motorola Razr 2024 Flip. It covers an overview of its features, navigating Motorola's user interface, customizing the operating system, and exploring built-in Google services.

Overview of Android 14 Features

Android 14 brings a host of new features designed to improve performance, usability, and personalization. One of the most notable updates is its focus on user customization. Android 14 allows you to personalize nearly every aspect of your device, from themes and icons to font styles and color palettes, enabling you to create a look and feel that suits your preferences.

Another standout feature is the improved battery management system. Android 14 optimizes background processes and app activity to reduce battery consumption, helping the Motorola Razr 2024 Flip achieve longer usage times. Coupled with the device's 4200mAh battery and TurboPower charging, this ensures you stay connected throughout the day.

Privacy and security have also been enhanced. Android 14 introduces a centralized Privacy Dashboard, which lets you review and manage app permissions, track data access, and ensure your information remains secure. For instance, you can now grant temporary permissions to apps, ensuring they only access your data when actively in use.

Performance improvements are another key aspect of Android 14. The operating system is optimized for devices like the Motorola Razr 2024 Flip, delivering smoother animations, faster app launches, and better multitasking capabilities. These enhancements ensure that the foldable screen experience remains fluid and responsive.

Lastly, Android 14 emphasizes accessibility with features like magnification gestures, customizable text size, and text-to-speech improvements. These tools make the device more inclusive, catering to users with varying needs and preferences.

Navigating the Motorola User Interface

The Motorola Razr 2024 Flip features a customized user interface built on top of Android 14. This interface retains the clean, intuitive design of stock Android while adding Motorola-specific enhancements to improve usability and functionality.

When you unlock the device, you'll notice the main home screen is uncluttered, with app icons neatly arranged and a dock at the bottom for quick access to frequently used apps. Swiping up from the bottom of the screen opens the app drawer, where all installed apps are displayed in alphabetical order. You can swipe down from the top of the screen to access the Quick Settings panel, which includes toggles for Wi-Fi, Bluetooth, and brightness adjustments, as well as shortcuts to settings like "Do Not Disturb" and "Battery Saver."

Motorola's interface includes gestures that make navigation seamless. For example, you can swipe left or right to switch between open apps, or swipe up from the bottom to return to the home screen. If you prefer traditional buttons, you can enable them in the settings for navigation.

Unique to Motorola is the **Moto Actions** feature. These intuitive gestures allow you to perform actions quickly, such as twisting the phone twice to launch the camera, chopping twice to turn on the flashlight, or flipping the device face down to enable Do Not Disturb mode. These gestures are highly customizable, making them an efficient way to interact with the phone.

Another useful addition is the Moto Display. This feature enhances the Always-On Display by showing notifications, time, and battery status in a low-power mode. You can interact with notifications directly from this screen, dismissing or opening them without unlocking the device.

One of the strengths of Android 14 is its extensive customization options, allowing you to tailor the Motorola Razr 2024 Flip to your personal preferences. You can start by customizing the home screen. Long-press any empty space on the home screen to access options for changing wallpapers, adding widgets, and adjusting the layout. Choose from Motorola's pre-installed wallpapers or use your own photos to give the device a unique look.

Next, explore the **Material You** feature, which adjusts the system-wide color scheme based on your chosen wallpaper. The colors are applied to app icons, menus, and widgets, creating a cohesive and aesthetically pleasing interface.

You can also customize the lock screen by adding shortcuts to frequently used apps, such as the camera or phone dialer. This enables quick access to these functions without unlocking the device.

For deeper personalization, navigate to the Settings app, where you can adjust sound profiles, enable dark mode, or choose different fonts and icon shapes. Android 14 also allows you to rearrange the Quick Settings panel, letting you prioritize the toggles you use most often.

If you want more control over your device, enable Developer Options in the settings. This advanced menu allows you to tweak animations, USB debugging, and other technical features. However, make changes cautiously, as these options are intended for experienced users.

Exploring Built-In Google Services

The Motorola Razr 2024 Flip comes preloaded with Google's suite of services, which integrate seamlessly with Android 14. These services provide everything from productivity tools to entertainment options, making them an essential part of the device.

Google Assistant is one of the standout features, allowing you to control your phone using voice commands. You can ask it to send texts, set reminders, check the weather, or control smart home devices. To activate Google Assistant, simply say "Hey Google" or press and hold the power button.

Gmail, Google Calendar, and Google Drive are preinstalled, ensuring you can manage emails, schedule appointments, and store files in the cloud effortlessly. These apps sync automatically with your Google account, providing a seamless experience across devices.

The Play Store gives you access to millions of apps, games, movies, and books. Whether you're looking for social media platforms, productivity tools, or entertainment apps, the Play Store has you covered.

Google Photos is another powerful tool, offering unlimited cloud storage for photos and videos. Its advanced search capabilities make it easy to find specific images, while the editing tools allow you to enhance your pictures directly within the app.

For navigation, Google Maps provides detailed directions, real-time traffic updates, and recommendations for nearby restaurants, shops, and attractions. The integration with the external display of the Razr 2024 Flip means you can access basic navigation controls without unfolding the device.

YouTube and YouTube Music offer endless entertainment options, whether you're watching tutorials, listening to music, or streaming your favorite shows.

Lastly, Google Keep is a handy app for taking notes, creating to-do lists, and setting reminders. Its simplicity and cross-platform synchronization make it a valuable tool for productivity.

By exploring and utilizing these built-in Google services, you can enhance your experience with the

Motorola Razr 2024 Flip, making it a powerful tool for work, entertainment, and daily life.

Customizing Your Razr

One of the most exciting aspects of the Motorola Razr 2024 Flip is the ability to make it uniquely yours. Customization is a key feature of Android 14, allowing you to tailor the device to suit your preferences and daily needs. From changing themes and wallpapers to organizing the home screen, adding widgets, and managing notifications, this chapter covers everything you need to know about personalizing your Razr for maximum convenience and efficiency.

Changing Themes and Wallpapers

The look and feel of your phone play a significant role in how enjoyable it is to use. With Android 14 on the Motorola Razr 2024 Flip, you have countless options for changing themes and wallpapers to match your style or mood.

To start, long-press on any empty space on your home screen. This will open a menu where you can choose "Wallpaper & Style." Here, you'll find a variety of preloaded wallpapers designed to complement the vibrant pOLED display. Select from categories like nature, abstract art, or geometric patterns. You can also use your own photos as wallpapers, allowing you to personalize the device further with memories or favorite images.

In addition to wallpapers, you can explore the Material You design feature. This Android 14-exclusive option allows the system to automatically create a color palette based on your chosen wallpaper. The colors are applied system-wide, including the notification shade, settings menu, and compatible app interfaces, creating a cohesive and visually appealing design.

For users who enjoy changing themes frequently, you can download additional themes from the Google Play Store. Many themes come with unique icon packs, widgets, and font styles to completely transform the appearance of your phone. Switching between themes is easy and can be done in just a few taps.

Personalizing Home Screen Layouts

The home screen is the heart of your device, and personalizing it can make navigation quicker and more intuitive. The Motorola Razr 2024 Flip offers flexible home screen layout options to organize your apps, widgets, and shortcuts effectively.

Start by arranging your apps. Long-press an app icon to move it around the screen. Group similar apps into folders by dragging one app on top of another. For example, you can create a "Social" folder for apps like Instagram, Twitter, and TikTok or a "Work" folder for productivity tools like Gmail, Google Drive, and Calendar. Once created, folders can be renamed to suit their purpose.

You can adjust the grid size of the home screen to fit more or fewer icons. Open the "Home Settings" menu by long-pressing the home screen and selecting "Home Screen Layout." From here, choose a grid size that matches your preference, such as 4x5 or 5x6. Larger grids allow you to fit more apps, while smaller grids create a cleaner look.

For quick access to frequently used apps, add them to the dock at the bottom of the screen. The dock remains visible as you swipe through different home screen pages, making it a convenient spot for apps you use regularly.

Another useful feature is enabling or disabling the Google Discover page, which appears when you swipe right on the home screen. This page provides personalized news, weather updates, and recommended content based on your interests. You can turn it on or off in the home screen settings, depending on whether you find it helpful.

Using Widgets for Convenience

Widgets are a powerful way to add functionality and convenience to your home screen. These small, interactive tools provide quick access to information and app features without needing to open the app itself. The Motorola Razr 2024 Flip supports a wide variety of widgets, allowing you to customize your home screen with useful tools.

To add a widget, long-press on an empty area of the home screen and select "Widgets" from the menu.

You'll see a list of available widgets organized by app. Browse through the options and choose widgets that match your needs. For example:

- **Clock and Weather Widgets**: Keep track of the time and current weather conditions at a glance.
- **Calendar Widgets**: View upcoming appointments and events directly on your home screen.
- **Music Player Widgets**: Control your music playback without opening the app.
- **Fitness Widgets**: Track steps, calories burned, or activity goals if you use health apps.

Once you've selected a widget, drag it to your desired location on the home screen. Many widgets are resizable, so you can adjust their dimensions by long-pressing and dragging the edges. This allows you to fit multiple widgets on a single screen without overcrowding it.

Widgets are not only practical but also contribute to the aesthetic of your home screen. Experiment with different layouts and combinations to find a setup that balances form and function.

Managing notifications effectively is crucial to staying organized and avoiding unnecessary distractions. The Motorola Razr 2024 Flip provides extensive options for customizing how notifications appear and behave, ensuring you're only alerted to what matters most.

To configure notifications, go to "Settings" and select "Notifications." From here, you can manage notification settings for individual apps. For example, you can allow important apps like messaging platforms to send alerts while silencing less critical ones.

Android 14 also includes a feature called Notification Categories. This allows you to customize specific types of notifications within an app. For instance, in a messaging app, you can enable alerts for personal chats but mute group notifications. Simply tap on the app in the notifications settings to explore these options.

The Razr's external display also offers notification customization. You can choose which apps display notifications on the cover screen and how they appear. This is particularly useful for quickly checking messages or updates without unfolding the device.

For added control, enable the "Do Not Disturb" mode during specific times or activities. This feature silences all notifications except those from selected contacts or apps. You can schedule Do Not Disturb to activate automatically during bedtime, meetings, or workouts.

To avoid notification overload, use Android's snooze feature. Swipe left or right on a notification and tap the clock icon to snooze it for a set period. This allows you to focus on tasks without permanently dismissing important alerts.

By customizing notifications to suit your lifestyle, you can stay informed while minimizing interruptions, ensuring a smoother and more productive experience with your Motorola Razr 2024 Flip.

Customizing your Motorola Razr 2024 Flip not only makes it visually appealing but also enhances its functionality to fit your daily routine. Whether it's changing wallpapers, organizing the home screen, adding widgets, or managing notifications, these customization options ensure your device works the way you want it to.

Exploring Foldable Display Technology

The Motorola Razr 2024 Flip's foldable display technology is one of its standout features, offering users a unique blend of innovation, style, and functionality. With its combination of a vibrant pOLED main screen and a practical external cover screen, the device delivers versatility and an enhanced user experience. This chapter delves into optimizing the main screen, customizing the cover screen widgets, adopting best practices for the foldable design, and maintaining the display to ensure long-term durability and performance.

Optimizing the pOLED Main Screen

The 6.9-inch pOLED main screen is the centerpiece of the Motorola Razr 2024 Flip, delivering Full HD+ resolution (2640 x 1080 pixels), HDR10+ support, and a smooth 144Hz refresh rate. To get the most out of this stunning display, it's important to optimize its settings based on your preferences and usage habits.

Start by adjusting the **brightness levels**. The phone's adaptive brightness feature automatically adjusts the screen's brightness based on your environment. This is especially useful when moving between indoor and outdoor settings. However, if you prefer manual control, you can disable adaptive brightness and set your preferred level in the "Display" settings.

Next, customize the **color profile** to enhance your viewing experience. Motorola provides options like "Natural," "Boosted," and "Saturated" under the display settings. The "Natural" mode offers accurate color reproduction, while "Boosted" and

"Saturated" provide more vibrant and vivid visuals, making them ideal for watching movies or playing games.

Enable **Dark Mode** for a more comfortable viewing experience in low-light environments. Dark Mode not only reduces eye strain but also conserves battery life by utilizing the energy efficiency of the pOLED technology.

For gamers and those who enjoy fast-paced content, the 144Hz refresh rate ensures smooth motion and fluid animations. While the high refresh rate provides an exceptional experience, you can lower it to 60Hz or 90Hz in the settings to save battery during less demanding tasks.

To prevent accidental touches, especially when using the foldable display in cramped spaces, enable "Accidental Touch Protection." This feature reduces unintended interactions by ignoring touches near the screen edges.

Customizing the Cover Screen Widgets

The 3.6-inch cover screen is a game-changer, offering quick access to essential information and features without unfolding the device. Customizing this screen ensures it meets your daily needs and enhances convenience.

Begin by selecting the widgets you want to display. Long-press on the cover screen to enter customization mode, where you can add, rearrange, or remove widgets. Some popular widget options include:

- **Weather**: Stay updated with real-time weather conditions and forecasts.
- **Music Controls**: Control playback without opening the main screen.
- **Calendar**: View upcoming appointments and events at a glance.
- **Fitness Stats**: Sync with apps like Google Fit to track your activity.

You can also customize the shortcuts that appear on the cover screen. These shortcuts allow you to quickly access apps like the camera, messages, or flashlight. To configure them, go to the "Cover Screen Settings" menu in the device's settings.

The cover screen also serves as a viewfinder for the rear camera, enabling high-quality selfies. To use this feature, activate the camera from the cover screen and position the device as needed. You can even apply filters or adjust camera settings directly from the external display.

For further personalization, explore the available themes and layouts for the cover screen. Some themes allow you to display animations or interactive wallpapers, adding a touch of creativity to your device.

Best Practices for Using the Foldable Display

The foldable design of the Motorola Razr 2024 Flip introduces new ways to interact with your device. By adopting a few best practices, you can make the most of this innovative technology while keeping the display in top condition.

One of the key features of the foldable design is the ability to use the phone in **Flex View mode**. This mode allows the device to remain partially folded, creating a hands-free viewing experience. For example, you can prop the phone up on a table to watch videos, participate in video calls, or follow recipes while cooking. This eliminates the need for additional accessories like stands or holders.

When using the foldable display, be mindful of the hinge. Avoid excessive force when opening or closing the phone, as the hinge is designed to operate smoothly with minimal pressure. Use both hands to open the device evenly, which helps distribute the pressure and prolongs the hinge's lifespan.

Switch between the main and cover screens seamlessly by enabling "Display Continuity" in the settings. This feature ensures that the content you're viewing on the main screen continues on the cover screen when you close the device, and vice versa. It's especially useful when multitasking or quickly switching between tasks.

For gaming and entertainment, take advantage of the wide screen by enabling full-screen mode in compatible apps. This provides an immersive experience, making the most of the display's size and clarity.

Maintaining Screen Longevity

Foldable displays require special care to ensure they remain functional and visually appealing over time. The Motorola Razr 2024 Flip's pOLED screen is durable, but following a few maintenance tips can help extend its lifespan.

First and foremost, avoid applying unnecessary pressure to the screen. Unlike traditional glass screens, foldable displays are made of flexible materials that can be sensitive to sharp objects or excessive force. When cleaning the screen, use a microfiber cloth and gently wipe in a circular motion to remove fingerprints and smudges. Avoid using abrasive cleaning agents or rough materials that could scratch the surface.

To protect the screen, use the case provided by Motorola or purchase a third-party case designed specifically for foldable devices. These cases are engineered to accommodate the folding mechanism without interfering with its functionality.

Be cautious when using the phone in environments with extreme temperatures. High heat or freezing cold can affect the flexibility of the screen materials, potentially causing damage. Keep the device away from direct sunlight for extended periods, and avoid leaving it in hot cars or near heat sources.

Motorola has designed the hinge to withstand thousands of folds, but it's still a good idea to treat it gently. Avoid flipping the phone open or shut too quickly or forcefully, as this could strain the hinge mechanism over time.

Finally, enable "Screen Care Tips" in the settings to receive occasional reminders about best practices for maintaining the display. These tips are designed to help users avoid common mistakes that could lead to damage.

By optimizing the main screen, customizing the cover screen widgets, and adopting best practices for using and maintaining the foldable display, you can enjoy the full benefits of the Motorola Razr 2024 Flip's innovative design. Taking care of the screen not only ensures its longevity but also enhances your overall experience with this cutting-edge device.

Camera Features and Settings

The Motorola Razr 2024 Flip is equipped with a sophisticated dual rear camera system that delivers exceptional photography and video capabilities. With advanced features such as portrait mode, macro functionality, and low-light optimization, this camera system empowers users to capture stunning visuals in any scenario. This chapter provides a detailed guide to understanding and using the dual rear camera, mastering special modes, improving low-light photography, and recording high-quality videos.

Using the Dual Rear Camera

The Motorola Razr 2024 Flip features a powerful dual rear camera system consisting of a 50MP primary sensor and a 13MP ultra-wide/macro sensor. Each camera is designed to excel in specific scenarios, ensuring versatility for various types of photography.

The **50MP main camera** is the primary workhorse, offering a large f/1.7 aperture that allows more light to enter the sensor. This results in bright, clear, and detailed photos, even in challenging lighting conditions. The inclusion of Optical Image Stabilization (OIS) ensures that handheld shots remain sharp and free of blur caused by minor movements. This makes it ideal for everyday photography, from landscapes to group photos.

The **13MP ultra-wide/macro sensor** adds a new dimension to your photography. With a 120-degree field of view, the ultra-wide lens is perfect for capturing expansive landscapes, architecture, or large group shots. When switched to macro mode, the same sensor allows you to focus on subjects as close as a few centimeters, revealing intricate details in flowers, insects, or textures.

To switch between cameras, simply open the camera app and use the zoom slider or tap on the "Wide" and "Macro" icons. The camera app's user interface is intuitive, displaying options such as zoom levels, aspect ratios, and HDR settings. For everyday use, keep HDR (High Dynamic Range) enabled to balance highlights and shadows in your photos, ensuring evenly exposed images.

Mastering Portrait and Macro Modes

The Razr 2024 Flip's portrait mode and macro mode are standout features for creative photography. These modes allow you to experiment with focus and depth, making your images more engaging and professional-looking.

Portrait Mode is designed to create a shallow depth-of-field effect, where the subject is sharply in focus while the background is blurred. This effect, also known as bokeh, is ideal for capturing portraits of people, pets, or objects. To activate portrait mode, open the camera app and select the "Portrait" option. Position your subject within the frame, ensuring adequate distance from the background for optimal separation.

While shooting in portrait mode, you can adjust the intensity of the background blur using the on-screen slider. Experiment with this setting to achieve the desired level of bokeh. For the best results, ensure your subject is well-lit and stands out from the background. The camera's AI also detects faces and applies enhancements like skin smoothing and eye brightening, creating flattering portraits with minimal effort.

Macro Mode, on the other hand, is designed for extreme close-ups. Switch to macro mode by tapping the "Macro" icon in the camera app. This mode is perfect for capturing fine details that are often overlooked, such as the veins on a leaf, the texture of fabric, or the intricate design of jewelry.

To achieve the best results in macro mode, ensure the subject is well-lit and hold the camera steady. The ultra-wide/macro lens performs best when the subject is within its optimal focus range, typically a few centimeters away. Use a tripod or prop the phone on a stable surface to eliminate any camera shake during close-up shots.

Low-Light and Night Photography

Taking photos in low-light conditions can be challenging, but the Motorola Razr 2024 Flip's camera system is designed to excel in such scenarios. The 50MP main sensor, combined with advanced image processing algorithms, ensures that photos remain bright and detailed even in dim environments.

For general low-light photography, enable the **Night Vision** mode in the camera app. This mode uses multiple exposures to capture more light, resulting in bright, noise-free images with enhanced details. Night Vision works best when the phone is held steady, so consider using a tripod or resting the device on a stable surface.

When shooting in low light, pay attention to the available light sources. Position your subject near streetlights, candles, or other light sources to create interesting highlights and shadows. Avoid using the built-in flash unless absolutely necessary, as it can produce harsh lighting and unflattering shadows.

If you're photographing landscapes or cityscapes at night, use the ultra-wide lens to capture a broader view. The camera app also includes manual controls under the "Pro" mode, allowing you to adjust settings like ISO and shutter speed for more precise control. Lower ISO settings reduce noise, while slower shutter speeds allow more light to reach the sensor. Be sure to use a stable surface to prevent motion blur when using slow shutter speeds.

The Motorola Razr 2024 Flip is not only a capable photography tool but also excels in video recording. It supports 4K video at 30fps and Full HD at up to 60fps, offering flexibility for different recording scenarios.

To start, select the desired resolution and frame rate in the video settings. Higher resolutions like 4K provide exceptional detail, making them ideal for capturing scenic views or important moments. If you're recording fast-moving subjects, such as sports or pets, opt for 60fps for smoother motion.

Take advantage of **Optical Image Stabilization (OIS)** and Electronic Image Stabilization (EIS) to minimize shakiness in your videos. These features ensure stable footage even when recording handheld. For additional stability, consider using a gimbal or tripod for professional-grade results.

The ultra-wide lens is particularly useful for dynamic shots, such as action scenes or vlogs, as it captures a broader perspective. You can also use the main camera for close-up shots, switching between lenses seamlessly during recording for cinematic effects.

Audio quality is just as important as video quality, and the Razr's multiple microphones ensure clear sound capture. However, if you're recording in a noisy environment, consider using an external microphone for better audio isolation.

For creative projects, explore the **slow-motion** and **time-lapse** modes. Slow-motion is perfect for capturing dramatic moments like splashing water or falling objects, while time-lapse condenses long events into short, engaging videos.

Lastly, use the camera app's manual controls in "Pro Video" mode for advanced settings like focus peaking, exposure lock, and white balance adjustments. These tools allow you to fine-tune your recordings and achieve professional-quality results.

Mastering the camera features and settings on the Motorola Razr 2024 Flip unlocks endless possibilities for creativity and storytelling. Whether you're capturing stunning portraits, exploring the macro world, or recording cinematic videos, this device equips you with the tools to express your vision in extraordinary ways.

✳ *Elara Technova*

Productivity Tools and Features

The Motorola Razr 2024 Flip is more than just a stylish and innovative smartphone; it's also a powerful tool for boosting productivity. With its versatile features, foldable design, and access to a wide range of apps, this device can help you stay organized, multitask efficiently, and achieve your work or study goals. This chapter explores how to set up and optimize productivity tools, use multitasking features like split-screen mode, integrate the Razr into your work and study routine, and select the best apps to maximize efficiency.

Setting Up Email and Calendar Apps

Managing your email and schedule is one of the most essential productivity tasks, and the Motorola Razr 2024 Flip makes it easy to stay organized. The device comes preloaded with the Gmail app, but you can also download other email clients like Microsoft Outlook, Yahoo Mail, or Spark from the Google Play Store if you prefer.

To set up your email account, open your preferred email app and follow these steps:

1. **Add Your Email Account**: Enter your email address and password. For work accounts, you may need to enter additional server settings, which can be obtained from your IT department.
2. **Sync Your Emails**: Choose how frequently you want the app to sync your emails. Frequent syncing ensures you receive emails in real-time but may consume more battery.
3. **Organize Your Inbox**: Use features like labels, folders, or categories to sort your emails. For

instance, you can create folders for work, personal, and promotional emails.

4. **Enable Notifications**: Customize notifications to ensure you're alerted to important emails without being overwhelmed by unnecessary alerts.

The Calendar app is another powerful tool for managing your schedule. Open the Google Calendar app or download alternatives like Microsoft Outlook or Any.do Calendar for additional features. Use the calendar to:

- Schedule meetings and appointments.
- Set reminders for important deadlines.
- Sync events from multiple accounts, such as work and personal calendars.
- Create recurring events for regular tasks or meetings.

By integrating your email and calendar apps, you can receive meeting invitations, RSVP directly from your inbox, and get notified about upcoming events. This seamless connection ensures you stay on top of your tasks and commitments.

Multitasking with Split-Screen Mode

The Motorola Razr 2024 Flip's foldable design and large main display make multitasking incredibly convenient. One of the best ways to enhance productivity is by using the split-screen mode, which allows you to run two apps simultaneously.

To activate split-screen mode:

1. Open the first app you want to use.
2. Swipe up from the bottom of the screen to access the Recent Apps view.
3. Tap the three-dot menu on the app window and select "Split Screen."
4. Choose the second app you want to open from the list of recent apps or the app drawer.

Once in split-screen mode, you can adjust the size of each app window by dragging the divider between them. This flexibility is particularly useful for tasks like:

- **Taking Notes While Browsing**: Open a note-taking app on one side and a web browser on the other to jot down ideas or research findings.
- **Responding to Emails During Video Calls**: Keep your video call running in one window while drafting an email in the other.
- **Comparing Documents**: View two PDFs or Word documents side by side for easy comparison.

The split-screen mode is a game-changer for multitasking, especially for users who need to balance multiple tasks efficiently. It allows you to stay focused and complete tasks faster without constantly switching between apps.

Using the Razr for Work and Study

The Motorola Razr 2024 Flip is an excellent tool for professionals and students alike. Its compact design, combined with powerful hardware and software, makes it ideal for work and study purposes.

For professionals, the Razr supports essential productivity apps like Microsoft Office, Google Workspace, and Slack. You can create and edit documents, spreadsheets, and presentations directly on your device. The foldable design also allows you to prop the phone up in Flex View mode during video calls, making it hands-free and convenient for virtual meetings.

Students can benefit from apps like Google Classroom, Evernote, and Quizlet to stay organized and on top of their coursework. The Razr's split-screen mode is particularly useful for studying, as it allows you to watch lectures or tutorials on one side while taking notes on the other. Additionally, the device's large main display is perfect for reading eBooks, reviewing study materials, or annotating PDFs.

The Razr's 5G connectivity ensures fast internet speeds, enabling seamless collaboration on cloud-based platforms like Google Drive or Dropbox. Whether you're sharing files with colleagues or accessing group projects, the device's performance ensures that tasks are completed efficiently.

For added convenience, use the Motorola Ready For feature, which allows you to connect your phone to a monitor or TV. This transforms your Razr into a desktop-like experience, complete with support for a mouse and keyboard. It's perfect for situations where you need a larger screen or a more traditional workstation setup.

Best Apps for Boosting Productivity

The Google Play Store offers a wide range of productivity apps that can help you make the most of your Motorola Razr 2024 Flip. Here are some of the best apps to consider:

1. **Microsoft Office**: Create, edit, and share Word, Excel, and PowerPoint files.
2. **Google Drive**: Store and access your files in the cloud, with seamless integration with other Google apps.
3. **Trello**: Organize your tasks and projects with boards, lists, and cards. Perfect for team collaboration and personal planning.

4. **Evernote**: Take notes, create to-do lists, and save web clippings all in one place.
5. **Slack**: Communicate and collaborate with your team through channels, direct messages, and file sharing.
6. **Adobe Acrobat Reader**: View, annotate, and sign PDFs on the go.
7. **Zoom**: Host or join virtual meetings with HD video and audio.
8. **Forest**: Stay focused by growing virtual trees while working or studying. This app helps reduce distractions and boost productivity.
9. **Notion**: A versatile app for managing projects, taking notes, and creating databases.
10. **CamScanner**: Turn your phone into a portable scanner for digitizing documents, receipts, and notes.

These apps, combined with the Razr's features, create a powerful productivity ecosystem. By choosing the tools that align with your needs, you can transform your phone into a reliable companion for work, study, and everyday tasks.

The Motorola Razr 2024 Flip is not just a smartphone; it's a productivity powerhouse designed to simplify your life and help you achieve your goals. By setting up email and calendar apps, utilizing multitasking features, integrating the device into your routine, and selecting the best productivity apps, you can make the most of this innovative device and stay organized and efficient in every aspect of your life.

Gaming on the Motorola Razr 2024 Flip

The Motorola Razr 2024 Flip is not just a stylish foldable smartphone; it's also a powerful gaming device capable of delivering an immersive and enjoyable gaming experience. With its advanced hardware, vibrant display, and 144Hz refresh rate, the Razr is designed to handle a wide range of games, from casual to graphically demanding titles. This chapter explores how to set up Game Mode for an optimized experience, adjust graphics and performance settings, discover games that make the most of the foldable display, and choose the best accessories to enhance your gaming sessions.

Setting Up Game Mode

The Motorola Razr 2024 Flip comes equipped with a Game Mode feature that enhances gaming performance and minimizes distractions. Setting up Game Mode ensures you get a seamless gaming experience without interruptions from notifications, calls, or background processes.

To enable Game Mode, follow these steps:

1. Open the **Moto Gametime** app, which is designed to enhance your gaming experience.
2. Add the games installed on your device to the app. This ensures that the system recognizes when you're playing a game and applies optimizations automatically.
3. Customize Game Mode settings to suit your preferences. These settings include:
   o **Blocking Notifications**: Prevent calls, messages, and app notifications from interrupting your game.

- ○ **Performance Boost**: Allocate system resources to maximize game performance.
- ○ **Brightness Lock**: Prevent sudden changes in screen brightness during gameplay.
- ○ **Gesture Controls**: Disable accidental gestures like swiping or tapping that could disrupt your gaming session.

Game Mode also provides an in-game toolbar that can be accessed with a swipe. This toolbar allows you to record gameplay, take screenshots, monitor performance metrics, or toggle settings like Do Not Disturb without leaving the game.

By setting up Game Mode, you create a distraction-free environment where you can fully immerse yourself in your favorite games.

Optimizing Graphics and Performance

The Motorola Razr 2024 Flip is powered by a MediaTek Dimensity 7030 chipset, 8GB of RAM, and a 144Hz pOLED display, making it a strong contender for mobile gaming. To get the most out of your gaming sessions, optimizing graphics and performance is essential.

Start by adjusting the **graphics settings** in each game. Most modern games offer customizable settings for resolution, frame rate, and visual effects. Here's how to optimize these settings:

- **Resolution**: Choose a resolution that balances visual quality and performance. While the device can handle high resolutions, lowering the resolution slightly can improve frame rates in demanding games.
- **Frame Rate**: Set the frame rate to 60fps or higher for smoother gameplay. The Razr's 144Hz display can support higher refresh rates, but some games may require manual adjustment.
- **Visual Effects**: Disable or lower settings for shadows, reflections, and anti-aliasing if you experience lag or stuttering. These features consume significant resources and can affect performance.

To further optimize performance, close background apps before launching a game. This frees up system resources and ensures the phone focuses solely on the game. Additionally, enable **Battery Saver for Gaming** in the Game Mode settings to prevent overheating and extend battery life during extended sessions.

The Razr's advanced cooling system helps maintain consistent performance even during long gaming sessions. However, if you notice the device becoming warm, consider taking short breaks to let it cool down.

Best Games for Foldable Displays

The foldable design of the Motorola Razr 2024 Flip adds a unique dimension to mobile gaming. The large, immersive main display and versatile Flex View mode enhance the gameplay experience, especially for titles that take advantage of the expanded screen real estate.

Here are some of the best games to enjoy on the Razr's foldable display:

1. **Asphalt 9: Legends**: This high-octane racing game takes full advantage of the vibrant pOLED display, delivering stunning graphics and smooth gameplay.
2. **Call of Duty: Mobile**: The large screen makes it easier to spot enemies and navigate the map, giving you a competitive edge in this popular FPS game.
3. **Genshin Impact**: This open-world RPG looks breathtaking on the Razr's display, with vivid landscapes and detailed character models.

4. **PUBG Mobile**: The foldable screen provides a larger field of view, improving accuracy and situational awareness in this battle royale game.
5. **Monument Valley 2**: The beautiful visuals and innovative puzzles are even more captivating on the Razr's foldable display.
6. **Minecraft**: Build and explore your world with enhanced clarity and detail on the main screen.
7. **Stardew Valley**: This farming simulation game benefits from the Razr's screen size, making inventory management and exploration easier.

In Flex View mode, you can prop the device up for hands-free gameplay, which is particularly useful for turn-based strategy games, puzzles, or casual titles.

Gaming Accessories for the Razr

Enhancing your gaming experience with accessories can make a significant difference, especially for long gaming sessions. Here are some of the best accessories to consider for your Motorola Razr 2024 Flip:

1. **Gaming Controllers**: Attach a Bluetooth gaming controller like the Razer Kishi or SteelSeries Stratus+ to enjoy console-like gameplay. These controllers provide physical buttons and

joysticks, making them ideal for action and racing games.

2. **Cooling Pads**: While the Razr's cooling system is efficient, an external cooling pad can help maintain performance during intense gaming sessions. These pads prevent overheating and ensure smooth gameplay.

3. **Wireless Earbuds**: Invest in high-quality wireless earbuds like the Motorola VerveBuds or Bose QuietComfort Earbuds for immersive audio. The Razr supports low-latency audio, ensuring sound syncs perfectly with the on-screen action.

4. **Power Banks**: A portable power bank with fast-charging capabilities is essential for gaming on the go. Look for one with USB-C compatibility to charge your Razr quickly during extended play.

5. **Foldable Phone Stands**: Use a foldable stand to hold the Razr in place during hands-free gaming. This accessory is especially useful when using the Flex View mode for games that don't require constant input.

6. **Screen Protectors and Cases**: Protect the foldable display with a high-quality screen protector and a gaming-friendly case. Choose a case that doesn't obstruct the edges of the screen or the folding mechanism.

These accessories not only enhance your gaming experience but also ensure your device remains protected and functional during heavy use.

The Motorola Razr 2024 Flip combines innovative design and powerful performance to create an exceptional gaming experience. By setting up Game Mode, optimizing graphics, exploring games designed for foldable displays, and using the right accessories, you can elevate your mobile gaming sessions to a whole new level. Whether you're a casual gamer or a dedicated enthusiast, the Razr is a reliable companion for all your gaming adventures.

Maximizing Internet and Connectivity

The Motorola Razr 2024 Flip is a device built for seamless connectivity, offering cutting-edge features such as 5G support, Wi-Fi 6/6E compatibility, advanced Bluetooth pairing, and NFC functionality. These capabilities ensure that users stay connected at high speeds, interact effortlessly with other devices, and use their smartphone for a variety of tasks, from streaming to contactless payments. This chapter delves into the details of setting up and maximizing the Razr's connectivity features to enhance your daily experience.

Setting Up 5G on Your Razr

One of the standout features of the Motorola Razr 2024 Flip is its ability to support 5G networks, offering ultra-fast internet speeds and low latency. Whether you're streaming high-definition videos, playing online games, or participating in video calls, 5G ensures a smooth and responsive experience. Setting up 5G on your Razr is straightforward and involves a few simple steps.

First, ensure that your SIM card is 5G-enabled. Most mobile carriers now provide 5G-compatible SIMs, but you may need to contact your service provider to confirm. If your current SIM card does not support 5G, visit your carrier's store to upgrade it.

Once you have a 5G-enabled SIM, insert it into the SIM tray of your Razr using the SIM ejector tool. Power on the device and go to the **Settings** app. Navigate to **Network & Internet** and select **Mobile Network**. From here, ensure that the **Preferred Network Type** is set to 5G. The phone will automatically detect and connect to 5G networks whenever they are available.

Keep in mind that 5G coverage varies depending on your location. If you're in an area without 5G service, the Razr will automatically switch to 4G LTE for uninterrupted connectivity. Additionally, 5G networks consume more battery power than 4G, so consider enabling **Battery Saver** mode during prolonged usage.

With 5G, you can enjoy faster downloads, buffer-free streaming, and real-time communication, making it a transformative feature for both work and entertainment.

Wi-Fi 6/6E: What You Need to Know

Wi-Fi 6 and 6E are the latest advancements in wireless internet technology, designed to offer faster speeds, greater capacity, and improved efficiency compared to previous Wi-Fi standards. The Motorola Razr 2024 Flip is compatible with both, ensuring a superior internet experience when connected to a compatible router.

Wi-Fi 6 provides faster data rates, reduced latency, and better performance in crowded environments, such as apartments or offices with many connected devices. Wi-Fi 6E takes it a step further by utilizing the 6GHz band, which is less congested than the 2.4GHz and 5GHz bands. This results in even faster speeds and more reliable connections.

To take full advantage of Wi-Fi 6/6E on your Razr, you need a compatible Wi-Fi router. If you're using an older router, consider upgrading to one that supports these standards. Once your router is set up, follow these steps to connect your Razr:

1. Open the **Settings** app and go to **Network & Internet**.
2. Select **Wi-Fi** and toggle it on if it's not already enabled.
3. Choose your Wi-Fi network from the list of available options.
4. Enter the password and tap **Connect**.

For optimal performance, position your router in a central location, free from obstructions like walls or large furniture. If you experience weak signals in certain areas of your home, consider using Wi-Fi extenders or mesh systems to expand coverage.

With Wi-Fi 6/6E, tasks like streaming 4K videos, downloading large files, and participating in video conferences become faster and more reliable, even when multiple devices are connected to the same network.

Bluetooth connectivity is an essential feature for modern smartphones, enabling seamless interaction with wireless headphones, speakers, smartwatches, and more. The Motorola Razr 2024 Flip supports Bluetooth 5.4, offering faster pairing, lower power consumption, and extended range compared to older versions.

To pair a Bluetooth device with your Razr, follow these steps:

1. Open the **Settings** app and go to **Connected Devices**.
2. Tap **Pair New Device**. The Razr will begin searching for nearby Bluetooth devices.
3. Make sure the device you want to pair is in pairing mode. Refer to the device's user manual for specific instructions, as the method may vary.
4. Once the device appears on the list, tap its name to connect.
5. Follow any on-screen prompts, such as entering a passcode, to complete the pairing process.

Once paired, the device will automatically connect to your Razr whenever Bluetooth is enabled and the device is within range. You can view and manage all connected devices under the **Previously Connected Devices** section in the settings.

Bluetooth 5.4's extended range allows you to stay connected even if you move to another room, making it ideal for activities like listening to music while doing chores or taking calls on a wireless headset.

For a more immersive experience, explore features like **Dual Audio**, which lets you connect two Bluetooth devices simultaneously. This is perfect for sharing music with a friend or connecting both a headset and a speaker.

Using NFC for Payments

The Motorola Razr 2024 Flip includes NFC (Near Field Communication) technology, which enables contactless payments, file sharing, and even pairing with other NFC-enabled devices. One of the most common uses of NFC is mobile payments through platforms like Google Pay.

To set up NFC for payments:

1. Open the **Settings** app and go to **Connected Devices**.
2. Select **NFC** and toggle it on.

3. Download and set up Google Pay from the Google Play Store if you haven't already.
4. Add your credit or debit card details by following the app's instructions. This may include verifying your card through an SMS code or email from your bank.

Once set up, you can use NFC to make payments by holding your Razr near a contactless payment terminal. You'll typically hear a beep or see a confirmation message on the terminal screen when the payment is successful. NFC payments are secure, as they use tokenization to encrypt your card details, ensuring they're not shared with the merchant.

Beyond payments, NFC can be used for other tasks like sharing contact information, photos, or files with another NFC-enabled device. Simply enable NFC on both devices, bring them close together, and follow the prompts to complete the transfer.

NFC is also useful for pairing accessories, such as wireless speakers or headphones, without the need for manual Bluetooth pairing. Look for the NFC logo on the accessory and tap your phone against it to connect instantly.

The Motorola Razr 2024 Flip's advanced internet and connectivity features ensure you're always connected, whether you're browsing on 5G, streaming on Wi-Fi 6, pairing Bluetooth devices, or using NFC for payments. By understanding and utilizing these capabilities, you can unlock the full potential of your device and enhance your daily activities with speed, convenience, and reliability.

Audio Features and Customization

The Motorola Razr 2024 Flip is equipped with advanced audio features that ensure high-quality sound for calls, music, movies, and other forms of entertainment. Its audio capabilities can be further customized to match your preferences, whether you're using the phone's built-in speakers, wireless audio devices, or apps. This chapter explores how to adjust sound settings, effectively use wireless audio accessories, enhance audio quality for various scenarios, and identify the best audio apps to elevate your listening experience.

Adjusting Sound Settings

Customizing the sound settings on your Motorola Razr 2024 Flip allows you to tailor the audio output to your needs. The phone's audio settings are easily accessible and provide several options for optimizing sound quality.

To adjust the sound settings, go to the **Settings** app and select **Sound & Vibration**. From here, you can manage the following:

- **Volume Levels**: Separate sliders for media, calls, notifications, and alarms let you adjust the volume for different activities. For instance, you can keep media volume high while lowering notification tones to avoid distractions during video playback.
- **Do Not Disturb Mode**: This feature silences all alerts except those you specifically allow. Customize it to enable calls or messages from select contacts while blocking other sounds.
- **Ringtone and Notification Sounds**: Choose from preloaded ringtones or set a custom audio

file as your ringtone. You can also assign unique notification tones for individual apps.

- **Vibration Patterns**: If you prefer vibration alerts, customize the vibration intensity and patterns for calls and notifications.

The Razr also includes **Equalizer Settings**, which allow you to fine-tune the sound profile for your media. Access this feature under **Audio Effects** in the settings menu. You can adjust bass, treble, and midrange levels or select preset profiles such as "Rock," "Pop," or "Classical." These settings make it easy to optimize audio for different types of music or content.

Using Wireless Audio Accessories

The Motorola Razr 2024 Flip supports Bluetooth 5.4, enabling seamless pairing with wireless audio accessories such as earbuds, headphones, and speakers. Wireless audio provides freedom of movement while maintaining excellent sound quality, making it ideal for commuting, exercising, or relaxing at home.

To pair a Bluetooth audio device:

1. Open the **Settings** app and go to **Connected Devices**.

2. Tap **Pair New Device** to scan for nearby Bluetooth devices.
3. Put your audio accessory in pairing mode (refer to the device manual if needed).
4. Select the device name from the list on your Razr and follow any on-screen prompts to complete the pairing.

Once paired, the audio device will automatically connect to your Razr whenever Bluetooth is enabled and the accessory is within range. You can manage connected devices in the **Previously Connected Devices** section of the settings.

For enhanced functionality, explore **Advanced Bluetooth Settings** under the same menu. These settings allow you to:

- Enable **Dual Audio**, which lets you connect two Bluetooth devices simultaneously, such as sharing music with a friend or connecting to a speaker and headphones at the same time.
- Prioritize **Audio Quality or Latency**, depending on your use case. For example, choose high-quality audio for music or low-latency mode for gaming.

If you frequently switch between devices, such as moving from headphones to a car audio system, the

Razr's intuitive interface ensures smooth transitions without the need to re-pair devices.

Enhancing Audio for Calls and Media

The Motorola Razr 2024 Flip includes several features to improve audio clarity and quality during calls and media playback. These enhancements ensure that your experience is not only enjoyable but also free from distractions or distortions.

For **calls**, the Razr uses advanced noise reduction technology to filter out background sounds, making your voice clearer to the person on the other end. This is particularly useful in noisy environments such as cafes or public transport. To enable noise reduction, go to **Settings > Call Settings** and toggle the noise cancellation feature.

Additionally, the phone supports **HD Voice** for calls, which enhances audio clarity by transmitting a broader range of sound frequencies. Check with your carrier to confirm HD Voice compatibility and ensure it's activated on your plan.

When it comes to **media playback**, the Razr's stereo speakers deliver rich and immersive sound. The speakers are tuned to provide balanced audio with crisp highs, clear mids, and deep bass. If you prefer using headphones, the device supports high-resolution audio codecs such as aptX and LDAC, ensuring superior sound quality with compatible accessories.

For an even more immersive experience, enable **Dolby Atmos**, which creates a surround sound effect for movies, music, and games. You can activate Dolby Atmos in the **Audio Effects** menu and choose from presets like "Movie," "Music," or "Custom." This feature enhances spatial audio, making content feel more dynamic and lifelike.

Best Audio Apps for Entertainment

To further enhance your audio experience, the Google Play Store offers a wide variety of apps for music, podcasts, and other forms of entertainment. Here are some of the best apps to consider for your Motorola Razr 2024 Flip:

1. **Spotify**: One of the most popular music streaming platforms, Spotify offers millions of songs, curated playlists, and personalized recommendations.
2. **YouTube Music**: A versatile app for streaming music videos, albums, and live performances. It also allows offline downloads with a premium subscription.
3. **Audible**: Perfect for audiobook lovers, Audible provides a vast library of titles across various

genres. The app includes features like adjustable narration speed and bookmarks.

4. **Pocket Casts**: A highly-rated podcast app with a user-friendly interface, episode filters, and playback controls.
5. **Poweramp**: A feature-rich music player that supports various file formats and includes a built-in equalizer for customizing audio.
6. **TIDAL**: Known for its high-fidelity audio streaming, TIDAL is an excellent choice for audiophiles seeking superior sound quality.
7. **Shazam**: Quickly identify songs playing around you and add them to your favorite streaming app with just one tap.
8. **Wavelet**: A powerful equalizer app for headphone users, offering features like bass boost, virtualizer, and reverb controls.

These apps, combined with the Razr's audio features, allow you to enjoy music, podcasts, audiobooks, and more with exceptional clarity and convenience.

The Motorola Razr 2024 Flip's audio capabilities are designed to provide a premium listening experience for calls, music, and media. By adjusting sound settings, using wireless accessories, enhancing audio quality, and exploring the best entertainment apps, you can tailor the device to meet your audio preferences and make the most of its advanced technology. Whether you're relaxing at home or on the go, the Razr ensures you're always surrounded by exceptional sound.

Battery Management

The Motorola Razr 2024 Flip is equipped with a 4200mAh battery that combines efficiency and longevity to support your daily activities. Whether you're streaming videos, playing games, or staying connected on social media, proper battery management ensures your device runs smoothly throughout the day. This chapter provides a comprehensive guide to TurboPower charging, practical tips for optimizing battery performance, wireless charging best practices, and monitoring battery health to keep your phone in top condition.

TurboPower Charging Explained

TurboPower charging is Motorola's proprietary fast-charging technology designed to recharge your Razr quickly and efficiently. With the 30W TurboPower charger included in the box, you can significantly reduce charging time, allowing you to get back to using your device without long interruptions.

The Razr's fast-charging capabilities are especially useful for busy users who need a quick power boost during the day. For instance, a 10-15 minute charge can provide several hours of usage, depending on your activities. The charger is optimized to deliver maximum power during the initial phase of charging, filling the battery to around 50% in a short amount of time, and then gradually reducing the charging speed to protect the battery from overheating or overcharging.

To use TurboPower charging effectively, ensure you use the original charger and USB-C cable provided by Motorola. Third-party chargers may not deliver the same performance or could potentially harm the battery. Additionally, keep the charging port and cable clean and free of debris to ensure a stable connection.

It's important to note that TurboPower charging works best at room temperature. If the device or charger becomes too warm, the system may automatically slow down charging to prevent overheating. For this reason, avoid charging your phone in direct sunlight or on heat-retaining surfaces.

Tips for Battery Optimization

Maximizing battery life is essential to ensure your Motorola Razr 2024 Flip lasts throughout the day. By following simple battery optimization techniques, you can reduce unnecessary power consumption without compromising performance.

1. **Enable Battery Saver Mode**: Battery Saver reduces background activity, such as app refresh and push notifications, to extend battery life. You can enable it manually in the settings or set it to activate automatically when the battery level drops below a certain percentage.
2. **Adjust Display Settings**: The Razr's pOLED display is vibrant and power-efficient, but high brightness and long screen-on times can drain the battery. Use

adaptive brightness to let the phone adjust the brightness based on ambient light, and reduce the screen timeout duration to minimize idle usage.

3. **Close Background Apps**: Apps running in the background consume power even when not in use. Regularly check and close unused apps by accessing the recent apps menu.

4. **Disable Unused Features**: Turn off Wi-Fi, Bluetooth, GPS, and NFC when they're not needed. These features continuously search for connections and can drain the battery if left on unnecessarily.

5. **Use Dark Mode**: The Razr's pOLED display benefits from Dark Mode, which reduces power consumption by displaying darker colors. This is particularly effective for apps and system menus that support Dark Mode.

6. **Manage App Permissions**: Restrict apps from running in the background by managing their battery usage in the settings. Focus on apps that you rarely use or that consume significant power.

7. **Avoid Overcharging**: Modern smartphones, including the Razr, have mechanisms to prevent overcharging, but it's still a good idea to unplug the charger once the battery reaches 100%.

By adopting these practices, you can ensure that your Razr's battery remains reliable and lasts longer between charges.

Wireless Charging Best Practices

The Motorola Razr 2024 Flip supports wireless charging, providing a convenient and cable-free way to power up your device. Wireless charging works by transferring energy from a charging pad to your phone through electromagnetic induction. While this method is slower than TurboPower charging, it is highly practical for desk setups, bedside tables, and other stationary locations.

To use wireless charging:

1. Place the wireless charging pad on a flat surface.
2. Connect the charging pad to a compatible power adapter.
3. Position your Razr on the pad, ensuring the back of the phone aligns with the charging coil in the pad.

The device will display a charging notification or icon when it begins charging. To maximize efficiency and safety, use a wireless charger that meets the **Qi** standard, as this ensures compatibility and performance.

Keep in mind the following best practices for wireless charging:

- **Remove Thick Cases or Metal Attachments**: Thick phone cases, metal plates, or magnetic mounts can interfere with wireless charging. Remove these accessories before placing your phone on the pad.
- **Position Correctly**: Misalignment between the phone and the charging pad can result in slower charging or no charging at all. Adjust the phone's position until it starts charging properly.
- **Avoid Overheating**: Like wired charging, wireless charging generates heat. Ensure the charging pad is placed in a well-ventilated area and avoid using the phone heavily while it charges wirelessly.

Wireless charging is an excellent option for overnight charging or for keeping your phone topped up while working.

Monitoring Battery Health

Maintaining your battery's health is crucial for long-term performance. The Motorola Razr 2024 Flip includes built-in tools to monitor battery health and usage, helping you identify potential issues and optimize your charging habits.

To check your battery's health, go to **Settings >
Battery** and review the following:

- **Battery Usage**: This section shows which apps
  and processes are consuming the most power.
  If an app appears to be using excessive battery,
  consider adjusting its settings or limiting its
  background activity.
- **Screen Time**: View how long your screen has
  been active since the last charge. High screen
  usage can indicate the need to adjust display
  settings.
- **Charging History**: Some phones provide insights
  into charging patterns, such as how long the
  device has been charging and whether fast
  charging was used.

Motorola also includes smart charging features that
adapt to your habits to preserve battery health. For
instance, if you frequently charge your phone
overnight, the system may delay charging to 100%
until just before you wake up, reducing wear on the
battery.

If you notice that the battery drains unusually
quickly or fails to hold a charge, it may be time to
troubleshoot. Start by ensuring that your device is
running the latest software, as updates often include
battery optimizations. If the issue persists, consider
contacting Motorola support for further assistance.

By regularly monitoring your battery health and following recommended charging practices, you can ensure that your Razr continues to perform reliably for years to come.

The Motorola Razr 2024 Flip's battery management features are designed to provide both convenience and longevity. Whether you're taking advantage of TurboPower charging, optimizing battery usage, exploring wireless charging, or monitoring battery health, these practices will help you make the most of your device's power capabilities while maintaining its performance over time.

Integrating with Smart Home Devices

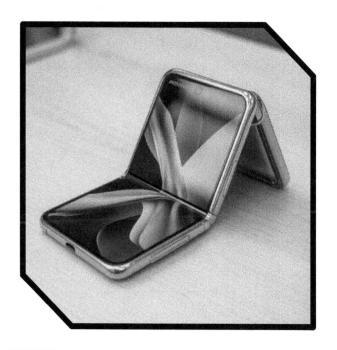

The Motorola Razr 2024 Flip is not just a communication and entertainment device; it's also a powerful tool for managing and integrating with smart home devices. Its compatibility with Google Home, Alexa, and various IoT platforms allows users to control lights, thermostats, security cameras, and more directly from their smartphone. This chapter provides a detailed guide on setting up Google Home integration, using Alexa with your Razr, controlling smart devices, and troubleshooting potential connection issues.

Setting Up Google Home Integration

Google Home is one of the most widely used platforms for managing smart home devices, and your Motorola Razr 2024 Flip makes the integration process seamless. To get started, you'll need the Google Home app, which is pre-installed on your Razr or available for download from the Google Play Store.

1. **Download and Open the Google Home App**: Launch the app and sign in with your Google account. If you don't have one, you'll need to create an account.
2. **Set Up Your Home**: Tap on "Set up device" and follow the on-screen instructions to create a "home." This virtual home will group all your smart devices for easy management.
3. **Add Devices**: If your smart devices are compatible with Google Home, they can be added by selecting "Works with Google" in the app. Choose your device brand from the list, log in to your device account, and link it to Google Home.

4. **Name and Assign Rooms**: Assign names and specific rooms to your devices. For example, label your smart light "Living Room Light" or your thermostat "Bedroom Thermostat." This organization makes voice commands and manual control more intuitive.
5. **Customize Settings**: Adjust individual device settings in the app, such as brightness levels for lights or temperature preferences for thermostats.

Once set up, you can control your devices using the Google Home app or Google Assistant. Simply say commands like, "Hey Google, turn on the living room lights," or "Hey Google, set the thermostat to 72 degrees." The integration ensures that all compatible devices work seamlessly with your Razr, making your smart home more accessible.

Using Alexa with Your Motorola Razr

For users who prefer Amazon's Alexa ecosystem, the Motorola Razr 2024 Flip offers full compatibility with Alexa-enabled devices. Whether you're using an Echo speaker, Fire TV, or Alexa-compatible smart gadgets, integrating them with your phone is straightforward.

1. **Install the Alexa App**: Download the Alexa app from the Google Play Store and sign in with your Amazon account.
2. **Set Up Your Devices**: Tap on the "Devices" tab in the Alexa app and select "Add Device." Follow the prompts to add and configure your smart devices.
3. **Enable Skills**: Alexa's "skills" enhance functionality for specific devices. Search for and enable skills related to your smart devices, such as "Philips Hue" for smart lights or "Ring" for security cameras. Log in to your device accounts to complete the linking process.
4. **Create Routines**: Use the Alexa app to create routines that automate tasks. For example, set a routine to turn off all lights and lock the doors with a single voice command like, "Alexa, goodnight."

Once integrated, you can control your devices using the Alexa app or voice commands. For instance, you can say, "Alexa, play my morning playlist," or "Alexa, show me the front door camera." With Alexa's extensive compatibility, your Razr becomes a central hub for managing your smart home.

Controlling Smart Devices from Your Razr

The Motorola Razr 2024 Flip simplifies the control of smart devices, allowing you to manage everything from lights to appliances directly from your phone. Here are some of the ways you can use your Razr to control your smart home:

- **Voice Commands**: Both Google Assistant and Alexa let you control devices hands-free. Simply use wake words like "Hey Google" or "Alexa," followed by your command.
- **Dedicated Apps**: Many smart devices have dedicated apps for advanced control. For example, use the Philips Hue app to customize lighting scenes or the Nest app to fine-tune thermostat settings.
- **Quick Settings Shortcuts**: Add smart device controls to your phone's Quick Settings menu for instant access. For example, toggle smart plugs or adjust lighting levels with a single tap.
- **Camera Monitoring**: Use your Razr to view live feeds from smart security cameras. Apps like Ring, Arlo, and Nest allow you to monitor your home from anywhere, providing peace of mind.
- **Smart Widgets**: Add widgets to your home screen for quick access to frequently used devices. For instance, create a widget to control your smart lights or view your thermostat settings without opening an app.

The foldable design of the Razr also enhances usability. You can prop the phone up in Flex View mode while adjusting smart devices or monitoring security feeds, freeing your hands for other tasks.

Troubleshooting Smart Home Connections

While the Motorola Razr 2024 Flip offers seamless integration with smart home devices, connection issues can occasionally arise. Here's how to troubleshoot common problems:

1. **Check Network Connectivity**: Ensure that both your Razr and smart devices are connected to the same Wi-Fi network. If the connection drops, restart your router and reconnect your devices.
2. **Update Software**: Outdated firmware on your smart devices or phone can cause compatibility issues. Check for updates in the respective apps and install them as needed.
3. **Re-Link Accounts**: If a device stops responding, unlink and re-link it to your Google or Alexa account. This often resolves issues caused by authentication errors.
4. **Verify Device Compatibility**: Not all smart devices work with Google Home or Alexa. Check the manufacturer's documentation to confirm compatibility and ensure you've enabled the correct skills or integrations.

5. **Reset Devices**: As a last resort, reset your smart device to its factory settings and set it up again. This can resolve persistent issues.

If problems persist, consult the help sections in the Google Home or Alexa apps, or contact the manufacturer's customer support for assistance.

The Motorola Razr 2024 Flip transforms your phone into a powerful tool for managing your smart home. By integrating with Google Home and Alexa, controlling devices directly from your Razr, and troubleshooting connections when needed, you can enjoy the convenience of a connected lifestyle with minimal effort. This integration not only simplifies daily tasks but also enhances the functionality and value of your smart home ecosystem.

Security and Privacy Features

The Motorola Razr 2024 Flip is designed with advanced security and privacy features to ensure that your personal data and sensitive information remain safe. With features like fingerprint and face unlock, secure folders, app permission management, and privacy best practices, you can confidently use your device without worrying about unauthorized access or data breaches. This chapter provides a detailed guide to setting up and using these features effectively.

Setting Up Fingerprint and Face Unlock

Securing your Motorola Razr 2024 Flip starts with enabling biometric authentication, which includes fingerprint scanning and face recognition. These methods are not only more convenient than traditional passwords but also provide an additional layer of security.

Setting Up Fingerprint Unlock:

1. Go to **Settings > Security > Fingerprint** and tap **Add Fingerprint**.
2. Follow the on-screen instructions to place your finger on the fingerprint sensor, which is embedded in the side-mounted power button.
3. Lift and reposition your finger as directed to capture different angles of your fingerprint.
4. Once the fingerprint is successfully registered, you can use it to unlock your phone, access apps, or authorize payments.

For optimal performance, register multiple fingerprints, such as your dominant hand and the opposite hand, to ensure quick access in various situations.

Setting Up Face Unlock:

1. Go to **Settings > Security > Face Unlock** and select **Set Up Face Recognition**.
2. Position your face within the frame on the screen and follow the prompts to complete the setup. Ensure you're in a well-lit environment for accurate scanning.
3. Once set up, you can unlock your phone simply by looking at it.

Face unlock works best in natural lighting and may not function well in low light or when wearing accessories like hats or glasses. For enhanced security, combine face unlock with another method, such as a PIN or fingerprint.

Protecting Your Data with Secure Folders

Secure Folders on the Motorola Razr 2024 Flip provide a private space to store sensitive files, photos, documents, and apps. This feature is especially useful for safeguarding data that you don't want accessible to anyone who might borrow or handle your phone.

Setting Up a Secure Folder:

1. Open the **Settings** app and navigate to **Security**.

2. Select **Secure Folder** and follow the instructions to set up the feature. You'll need to create a separate password, PIN, or pattern for accessing the secure folder.
3. Once set up, you can move files or apps into the secure folder. Simply select the items, tap **Move to Secure Folder**, and they'll be hidden from the main interface.

The secure folder is encrypted, meaning that even if your phone is lost or stolen, the data inside it remains inaccessible without the correct authentication. You can also customize the folder's appearance or hide it entirely from the app drawer for added privacy.

Configuring App Permissions Safely

Managing app permissions is critical for protecting your personal data. Many apps request access to features like your camera, microphone, location, and contacts, but not all require these permissions to function. Granting unnecessary permissions can expose you to privacy risks.

To configure app permissions:

1. Go to **Settings > Privacy > Permission Manager**.

2. Review the permissions by category (e.g., Location, Camera, Microphone) or by individual apps.
3. Tap on each app or category to adjust the permissions. You'll typically see options like **Allow All the Time, Allow Only While Using the App**, or **Deny**.

For example:

- Allow location access for navigation apps like Google Maps but deny it for games or unrelated apps.
- Restrict camera and microphone access to apps that genuinely need them, such as video call or photography apps.

In Android 14, the Motorola Razr 2024 Flip also includes a **Privacy Dashboard** that provides a summary of how often apps access sensitive features. Regularly reviewing this dashboard helps you identify apps that may be overstepping their bounds.

Best Practices for Privacy

Maintaining privacy on your Motorola Razr 2024 Flip goes beyond using built-in features. Following best practices ensures that your data remains secure in an increasingly connected world.

1. **Keep Software Updated**: Always install the latest system updates and security patches. These updates fix vulnerabilities and improve your phone's defenses against malware and other threats.
2. **Use Strong Passwords**: For apps and accounts, create unique passwords that are a combination of letters, numbers, and symbols. Avoid using easily guessed information like birthdays or names.
3. **Enable Two-Factor Authentication (2FA)**: For accounts like email, social media, and banking, enable 2FA to add an extra layer of protection. This requires a secondary verification step, such as a code sent to your phone.
4. **Avoid Public Wi-Fi**: When using public Wi-Fi networks, avoid accessing sensitive information like bank accounts or personal emails. If necessary, use a VPN to encrypt your connection.
5. **Be Cautious with Downloads**: Only download apps from trusted sources like the Google Play Store. Avoid third-party app stores, as they may host malicious software.
6. **Disable Bluetooth and NFC When Not in Use**: Keeping these features off prevents unauthorized connections or data transfers.
7. **Regularly Check App Activity**: Use the Privacy Dashboard to monitor app activity and revoke permissions for apps that don't need them.

8. **Lock Individual Apps**: Use third-party apps or built-in features to lock sensitive apps, like banking or social media, with a PIN or fingerprint.

Following these practices ensures that your personal information stays safe and that your Motorola Razr 2024 Flip remains secure against potential threats.

The Motorola Razr 2024 Flip is packed with advanced security and privacy features designed to protect your data and give you peace of mind. By setting up fingerprint and face unlock, using secure folders, managing app permissions, and adhering to privacy best practices, you can confidently use your device in today's digital landscape. These tools and habits make it easy to stay in control of your personal information while enjoying all the capabilities of your smartphone.

Troubleshooting Basics

The Motorola Razr 2024 Flip is designed to provide a seamless and reliable user experience, but like any advanced technology, it can encounter occasional issues. Whether it's a problem with Wi-Fi connectivity, screen display, overheating, or device performance, most issues can be resolved with simple troubleshooting steps. This chapter provides a comprehensive guide to fixing common problems, maintaining optimal performance, and knowing when a factory reset might be necessary.

Fixing Common Wi-Fi Issues

Wi-Fi connectivity issues are among the most common problems smartphone users face. Whether it's a slow connection, frequent disconnections, or difficulty connecting to a network, the Motorola Razr 2024 Flip offers tools and settings to help resolve these problems.

Steps to Troubleshoot Wi-Fi Issues:

1. **Check Your Wi-Fi Connection**: Ensure your router is functioning properly. Restarting your router often resolves minor connectivity issues.
2. **Toggle Wi-Fi**: Turn Wi-Fi off and back on to refresh the connection. You can do this from the Quick Settings menu or through **Settings > Network & Internet > Wi-Fi**.
3. **Forget and Reconnect to the Network**: If the problem persists, go to **Wi-Fi settings**, select the network, and choose **Forget Network**. Then reconnect by entering the password again.
4. **Restart Your Phone**: A simple restart can often fix connectivity problems by clearing temporary glitches in the system.

5. **Check for Software Updates**: Ensure your Razr's software is up to date. Updates often include fixes for known connectivity issues. Go to **Settings > System > Software Update** to check for updates.
6. **Reset Network Settings**: If none of the above works, reset your network settings. Go to **Settings > System > Reset Options > Reset Wi-Fi, Mobile & Bluetooth**. Note that this will erase all saved Wi-Fi networks and Bluetooth connections.

If the problem persists, test the phone with another Wi-Fi network to determine if the issue is with the phone or your router.

Resolving Screen Display Problems

The Motorola Razr 2024 Flip features a stunning pOLED foldable display, but issues like unresponsive touch, flickering, or unusual colors can occur. These problems are often easy to fix with a few adjustments or simple troubleshooting.

Steps to Address Display Issues:

1. **Check for Physical Damage**: Inspect the screen for visible cracks or scratches that might affect performance.

2. **Clean the Screen**: Use a soft, lint-free cloth to gently clean the screen. Dust or smudges can sometimes interfere with touch sensitivity.

3. **Restart the Phone**: A quick restart can often resolve temporary glitches. Hold down the power button and select **Restart**.

4. **Adjust Display Settings**: Go to **Settings > Display** to ensure the brightness, color mode, and refresh rate settings are correct. If the screen appears too dim or overly bright, disable adaptive brightness and adjust it manually.

5. **Check for App Issues**: Some third-party apps can cause display problems. Boot the phone in Safe Mode by holding the power button and long-pressing the **Power Off** option until **Safe Mode** appears. If the display works fine in Safe Mode, uninstall recently downloaded apps to identify the culprit.

6. **Update Your Software**: Display issues can sometimes result from software bugs. Check for updates in **Settings > System > Software Update**.

For persistent problems, such as dead pixels or significant touch unresponsiveness, contact Motorola support or visit an authorized service center for assistance.

Overheating or freezing can occur if the phone is under heavy use, such as running multiple apps, gaming, or streaming videos for extended periods. Proper management of usage and settings can prevent or resolve these issues.

Steps to Manage Overheating:

1. **Close Background Apps**: Running too many apps simultaneously can overwork the processor. Use the Recent Apps menu to close unnecessary apps.

2. **Avoid Direct Sunlight**: Prolonged exposure to heat, such as leaving the phone in a car or under direct sunlight, can cause overheating. Keep the phone in a cool, shaded place.

3. **Disable Power-Intensive Features**: Turn off Bluetooth, GPS, and 5G when not in use, as these can contribute to overheating.

4. **Use Battery Saver Mode**: Enable Battery Saver to reduce power consumption and lower the phone's temperature.

Steps to Address Freezing:

1. **Force Restart**: If the phone becomes unresponsive, hold down the power button and

volume down button simultaneously for about 10 seconds to force a restart.

2. **Clear Cache:** Go to **Settings > Storage > Cached Data** and clear the cache to remove temporary files that might be causing performance issues.

3. **Check for Problematic Apps:** Use Safe Mode to determine if a third-party app is causing the freezing. Uninstall recently added apps if the problem resolves in Safe Mode.

Regularly monitoring your device's temperature and usage can prevent overheating and freezing from becoming a recurring issue.

When to Perform a Factory Reset

A factory reset is a last-resort solution for persistent issues that cannot be resolved through other troubleshooting methods. This process restores the phone to its original factory settings, erasing all personal data, apps, and configurations.

When to Consider a Factory Reset:

- Persistent software bugs or glitches.
- Significant performance issues, such as frequent crashing or freezing.
- Difficulty removing malware or malicious apps.
- Preparing the phone for resale or gifting.

How to Perform a Factory Reset:

1. Back up your data. Go to **Settings > System > Backup** and ensure all important files, photos, and contacts are saved to Google Drive or another backup service.
2. Open **Settings > System > Reset Options** and select **Erase All Data (Factory Reset)**.
3. Confirm your selection and follow the on-screen instructions.

After the reset, the phone will reboot to its initial setup screen. You'll need to sign in with your Google account and reinstall apps.

Performing a factory reset can resolve deep-seated software issues, but it should only be done after trying other troubleshooting methods.

The Motorola Razr 2024 Flip is built to handle various challenges with ease, and this chapter equips you with the tools and knowledge to address common issues effectively. By following these troubleshooting steps, you can keep your device running smoothly and maintain its performance for years to come.

Elara Technova

Software Updates and Maintenance

Regular software updates and proper maintenance are essential for ensuring your Motorola Razr 2024 Flip runs smoothly, remains secure, and delivers the best performance. Staying up-to-date with the latest Android updates, keeping apps current, and performing routine maintenance tasks like clearing cache can significantly enhance your phone's usability and longevity. This chapter provides a detailed guide to installing Android updates, managing app updates, clearing cache, and scheduling regular maintenance to keep your device in top condition.

Installing Android Updates

Android updates play a critical role in maintaining your phone's security, introducing new features, and improving overall system performance. Motorola periodically releases updates to fix bugs, patch vulnerabilities, and enhance the user experience. Keeping your phone updated is one of the simplest yet most effective ways to ensure it performs optimally.

To check for and install Android updates on your Motorola Razr 2024 Flip, follow these steps:

1. Open the **Settings** app and navigate to **System**.
2. Tap **Software Update** to check if an update is available.
3. If an update is available, download it by tapping **Download and Install**. Ensure your device is connected to a Wi-Fi network and has at least 50% battery charge before proceeding.
4. Once the download is complete, follow the on-screen instructions to install the update. Your

phone will restart during the process, and the update will be applied.

Updates can vary in size, with some being minor patches and others being major Android version upgrades. Major updates may take longer to download and install, so plan accordingly. If your device is set to **Automatic Updates**, it will download updates in the background and prompt you to install them when convenient.

Installing updates promptly ensures that your phone remains secure and takes advantage of the latest advancements in Android technology. Delaying updates can leave your device vulnerable to security risks and may cause compatibility issues with newer apps.

Managing App Updates

Keeping your apps updated is just as important as maintaining your operating system. App updates often include bug fixes, performance enhancements, and new features that improve functionality. With the Motorola Razr 2024 Flip, managing app updates is simple and can be done through the Google Play Store.

To check for and update your apps:

1. Open the **Google Play Store** app and tap your profile icon in the top-right corner.
2. Select **Manage Apps & Device**.
3. Under the **Updates Available** section, you'll see a list of apps with pending updates.
4. Tap **Update All** to update all apps at once, or select individual apps to update them one by one.

To streamline the process, enable **Auto-Update Apps** in the Google Play Store settings. This ensures that apps update automatically when your phone is connected to Wi-Fi. However, if you prefer manual updates to save data or control the process, leave this option disabled.

Regularly updating your apps not only improves their performance but also ensures compatibility with your phone's latest software. Outdated apps can lead to crashes, slowdowns, or security vulnerabilities, so it's a good practice to check for updates frequently.

Clearing Cache for Improved Performance

Over time, apps and the system accumulate cached data, which can take up valuable storage space and potentially slow down your phone. Clearing the cache helps free up space and improve performance without deleting important data or settings.

There are two types of cache: **App Cache** and **System Cache**. Here's how to clear them:

Clearing App Cache:

1. Go to **Settings > Apps & Notifications**.
2. Select **See All Apps** to view a list of installed apps.
3. Tap on the app you want to clear the cache for.
4. Select **Storage & Cache**, then tap **Clear Cache**.

This process removes temporary files for that specific app without affecting your personal data.

Clearing System Cache:

1. Restart your phone in recovery mode by holding down the **Power** and **Volume Down** buttons simultaneously.
2. Use the volume buttons to navigate to **Wipe Cache Partition** and select it using the power button.
3. Confirm your selection and wait for the process to complete.

Clearing the system cache removes temporary system files that may be causing performance issues, such as slow boot times or lag. Perform this task periodically, especially after a major software update, to ensure smooth operation.

Proactive maintenance is key to extending the life of your Motorola Razr 2024 Flip and keeping it running at its best. Scheduling regular maintenance tasks ensures that small issues don't escalate into larger problems.

Here are some maintenance practices to include in your routine:

1. **Optimize Storage**: Regularly review your phone's storage usage by going to **Settings > Storage**. Delete unnecessary files, unused apps, and duplicate photos to free up space. Consider using cloud storage solutions like Google Drive or Google Photos to back up and manage your files.

2. **Run Device Health Checks**: Use the built-in Device Care feature to monitor your phone's performance, battery health, and storage status. Access this feature through **Settings > Device Care** or a similar section.

3. **Restart Your Phone Weekly**: Restarting your phone once a week clears temporary files and refreshes system processes, improving overall performance.

4. **Scan for Malware**: Install a reputable antivirus app from the Google Play Store to scan your phone periodically for potential threats. While

Android is generally secure, additional protection can safeguard against malicious apps and files.

5. **Inspect Hardware**: Check the phone's exterior for signs of wear, such as a loose charging port or damaged screen. Addressing hardware issues early prevents them from affecting performance.

By scheduling these tasks, you can ensure that your phone remains fast, efficient, and reliable for years to come.

The Motorola Razr 2024 Flip's software and maintenance tools are designed to keep your device performing at its best. Regular updates, cache clearing, app management, and proactive maintenance are simple yet effective steps to enhance your phone's longevity and functionality. Incorporating these practices into your routine will help you get the most out of your device while ensuring it remains secure and responsive.

Exploring the Brilliance of Foldable Tech

Foldable technology represents one of the most innovative advancements in the smartphone industry, combining style, functionality, and cutting-edge engineering. The Motorola Razr 2024 Flip is a testament to how far foldable tech has come, delivering a premium experience with its sleek design and robust performance. This chapter delves into the science behind foldable displays, the benefits of foldable smartphones, the durability improvements made in the Razr 2024 Flip, and the future potential of foldable technology.

The Science Behind Foldable Displays

Foldable displays are made possible through a combination of advanced materials and engineering techniques. Unlike traditional rigid screens, foldable displays use flexible polymers or ultra-thin glass (UTG) to create a screen that can bend and fold without breaking. The display on the Motorola Razr 2024 Flip features pOLED (Plastic OLED) technology, which is specifically designed to withstand repeated folding while maintaining vibrant colors, sharp resolutions, and high refresh rates.

The screen is layered with multiple components, including a flexible substrate, an OLED layer for vibrant visuals, and a protective coating. Each layer is engineered to be thin yet resilient, allowing the display to bend seamlessly while resisting wear and tear. The hinge mechanism is equally important in foldable phones. On the Razr 2024 Flip, the hinge is designed with precision to support the folding motion, reduce stress on the display, and eliminate visible creases when the phone is fully opened.

To enhance durability, Motorola incorporates advanced anti-scratch and anti-smudge coatings on the display. Additionally, the phone's software is optimized to detect and adapt to different screen orientations, ensuring a smooth transition between folded and unfolded states. The combination of these technologies creates an innovative, user-friendly experience that sets foldable smartphones apart from their traditional counterparts.

Benefits of Foldable Smartphones

Foldable smartphones offer unique advantages that make them appealing to a wide range of users. The Motorola Razr 2024 Flip, with its compact design and dual-display functionality, exemplifies these benefits.

One of the primary advantages of foldable phones is their ability to combine portability and functionality. When folded, the Razr 2024 Flip is compact enough to fit easily in your pocket or bag. When unfolded, it reveals a spacious main display that's perfect for watching videos, browsing the web, or multitasking. This versatility allows users to enjoy the best of both worlds without compromising on screen size or portability.

Foldable phones also enhance multitasking capabilities. With the Razr 2024 Flip's Flex View mode, you can prop the phone up at different angles for hands-free video calls, split-screen multitasking, or taking photos. The secondary cover display adds to the convenience by providing quick access to notifications, widgets, and essential tools without needing to open the phone.

Another benefit is the aesthetic appeal of foldable smartphones. The Razr 2024 Flip stands out with its iconic clamshell design, offering a sleek and modern look that distinguishes it from traditional phones. It's not just a functional device but also a statement piece that reflects innovation and sophistication.

Foldable phones also pave the way for new possibilities in app design and functionality. Many apps are now optimized for foldable displays, providing enhanced usability and creative features that take advantage of the larger screen real estate. From gaming to productivity, foldable smartphones open up new avenues for user engagement.

Durability Enhancements in the Razr 2024

Durability has always been a key consideration for foldable phones, and the Motorola Razr 2024 Flip introduces several advancements to address this challenge. The phone is designed to withstand the rigors of daily use, from repeated folding to exposure to environmental factors.

One of the standout features is the improved hinge mechanism, which is engineered for long-lasting performance. The hinge is reinforced with high-strength materials and precision components, allowing the phone to be folded thousands of times without degradation. Motorola has conducted rigorous durability tests to ensure the hinge remains smooth and reliable over time.

The pOLED display on the Razr 2024 Flip is another area where durability has been enhanced. The display is coated with multiple protective layers to resist scratches, smudges, and minor impacts. Additionally, the ultra-thin glass (UTG) used in the screen provides a balance of flexibility and strength, ensuring the display remains intact even after extensive use.

The phone also features a water-repellent design, which adds an extra layer of protection against accidental spills or light rain. While not completely waterproof, this coating helps protect the device's internal components from moisture damage. Motorola's commitment to durability makes the Razr 2024 Flip a reliable choice for users who value both style and longevity.

The foldable smartphone market is still in its early stages, but it holds immense potential for growth and innovation. The Motorola Razr 2024 Flip represents a significant milestone in this journey, showcasing what is possible when technology, design, and functionality come together.

In the future, foldable phones are expected to become more affordable and accessible, making them a viable option for a broader audience. As production costs decrease and manufacturing techniques improve, more brands will likely adopt foldable technology, leading to greater competition and innovation.

Technological advancements will also continue to enhance the durability and functionality of foldable devices. For instance, future models may feature even more resilient materials, longer-lasting hinges, and improved resistance to environmental factors like dust and water. Displays are expected to become thinner and more flexible, paving the way for creative designs such as rollable or stretchable screens.

Software optimization will play a crucial role in shaping the future of foldable technology. Developers are already creating apps and interfaces that adapt seamlessly to different screen orientations and sizes. This trend will only grow as foldable devices become more popular, offering users a richer and more interactive experience.

Foldable technology also has the potential to extend beyond smartphones. Laptops, tablets, and other devices could benefit from foldable displays, offering new possibilities for portability and functionality. As these technologies mature, they may redefine how we interact with our devices and integrate them into our daily lives.

The Motorola Razr 2024 Flip is a glimpse into the future of mobile technology, demonstrating the endless possibilities of foldable displays. With continued innovation, foldable technology is poised to transform the way we think about and use electronic devices, making it an exciting space to watch in the years to come.

The brilliance of foldable technology lies in its ability to combine innovation, practicality, and aesthetics into a single device. By understanding the science behind foldable displays, appreciating the benefits, exploring the durability enhancements, and looking ahead to future prospects, users can fully grasp the transformative potential of foldable smartphones like the Motorola Razr 2024 Flip. This is not just a phone; it's a glimpse into the future of technology.

Advanced Camera Tips

The Motorola Razr 2024 Flip is equipped with an advanced dual-camera system that makes it a powerful tool for photography and videography. With features like Pro Mode, high-quality editing tools, compatibility with camera accessories, and the ability to shoot cinematic videos, this device allows you to capture stunning images and videos with ease. In this chapter, we will explore how to unlock the full potential of the Razr's camera capabilities.

Pro Mode on the Motorola Razr 2024 Flip gives you full control over your camera settings, enabling you to capture professional-quality photos. Unlike the automatic mode, which adjusts settings for you, Pro Mode allows you to fine-tune elements such as ISO, shutter speed, white balance, focus, and exposure.

To access Pro Mode, open the camera app and select **Pro Mode** from the menu. Here's a breakdown of how to use its features:

- **ISO**: This controls the camera's sensitivity to light. Use a lower ISO (e.g., 100) for brightly lit environments and a higher ISO (e.g., 800 or above) for low-light conditions. However, higher ISO levels can introduce noise, so use them sparingly.
- **Shutter Speed**: Adjust the shutter speed to control motion blur. A fast shutter speed (e.g., 1/1000) freezes motion, ideal for capturing action shots, while a slower shutter speed (e.g., 1/30) creates motion blur, perfect for artistic effects like light trails.
- **White Balance**: White balance adjusts the color temperature of your photo. Choose between presets like daylight, cloudy, or tungsten to

match the lighting conditions and achieve accurate colors.

- **Manual Focus**: Pro Mode lets you adjust focus manually, which is useful for macro shots or when photographing subjects with intricate details. Slide the focus bar to sharpen specific areas of the image.
- **Exposure**: Use the exposure slider to brighten or darken your photo. This is especially helpful when shooting in challenging lighting conditions, such as backlit scenes.

Experimenting with these settings can help you create unique and visually striking photos. Practice using Pro Mode in different environments, such as landscapes, portraits, and night photography, to master the art of manual photography.

Editing Photos and Videos on Your Razr

Once you've captured stunning photos and videos, the Motorola Razr 2024 Flip provides a range of editing tools to refine your work. The built-in **Google Photos** app offers powerful editing features that are both user-friendly and effective.

Editing Photos:

1. Open the photo you want to edit in the Google Photos app.

2. Tap the **Edit** icon to access tools like cropping, rotating, and adjusting brightness, contrast, and saturation.
3. Use filters to enhance the mood of your photo. Choose from options like "Auto" for quick adjustments or "Drama" for a more dynamic look.
4. For precise editing, use the **Color and Light Adjustment** sliders to tweak shadows, highlights, warmth, and sharpness.

Editing Videos:

1. Open the video you want to edit and tap the **Edit** icon.
2. Trim unwanted parts by dragging the start and end points in the timeline.
3. Use the color adjustment tools to enhance brightness, contrast, and saturation.
4. Add music or captions to your video for a polished finish.

For more advanced editing, consider downloading third-party apps like Adobe Lightroom, Snapseed, or CapCut. These apps offer professional-grade tools for photo and video editing, allowing you to unleash your creativity and produce high-quality content.

Enhance your photography and videography experience with accessories designed to complement the Motorola Razr 2024 Flip. From external lenses to tripods, these tools can take your shots to the next level.

- **External Lenses**: Clip-on lenses, such as wide-angle, macro, or fisheye lenses, expand the camera's capabilities. A wide-angle lens is perfect for capturing expansive landscapes, while a macro lens lets you focus on intricate details in close-up shots.
- **Tripods and Stabilizers**: A sturdy tripod ensures steady shots, especially in low-light conditions or when shooting long exposures. For video recording, a gimbal stabilizer provides smooth, cinematic motion by minimizing hand tremors.
- **Portable Lighting**: Ring lights or LED panels are great for improving lighting in your photos and videos. They are especially useful for portraits or indoor shoots where natural light is limited.
- **Wireless Shutter Remote**: This accessory allows you to take photos remotely, which is ideal for group shots or long exposures.
- **Protective Cases**: Invest in a camera-friendly protective case that doesn't obstruct the lens. This ensures your device stays safe during outdoor shoots.

These accessories are widely available online and can significantly enhance the versatility and quality of your camera work.

Shooting Cinematic Videos

The Motorola Razr 2024 Flip's advanced camera system and video features make it ideal for creating cinematic videos. With the ability to shoot in 4K resolution and access advanced stabilization, you can produce professional-quality footage directly from your phone.

Tips for Shooting Cinematic Videos:

1. **Enable Stabilization**: The Razr includes electronic image stabilization (EIS) to reduce shakiness and create smoother footage. This is especially useful for handheld shots or when walking while filming.
2. **Use Manual Controls**: In Pro Mode, adjust settings like ISO, shutter speed, and white balance to achieve a cinematic look. For instance, use a slower shutter speed for natural motion blur or adjust the white balance to match the lighting.
3. **Experiment with Frame Rates**: The Razr supports different frame rates, such as 24fps for a classic cinematic feel or 60fps for smoother

motion. Choose the frame rate that best suits your creative vision.

4. **Focus on Composition**: Follow basic principles of composition, such as the rule of thirds, to frame your shots effectively. Use the gridlines feature in the camera app to guide your composition.

5. **Incorporate Movement**: Add dynamic motion to your videos by panning, tilting, or using slow zooms. Pair these techniques with a gimbal stabilizer for smooth transitions.

6. **Capture Sound Effectively**: Use an external microphone for better audio quality, especially when recording dialogue or ambient sounds. This can significantly improve the overall production value of your videos.

7. **Edit Your Footage**: After shooting, use editing apps to color-grade your video, add transitions, and overlay background music. Apps like KineMaster and Adobe Premiere Rush are excellent for mobile video editing.

By combining these techniques, you can create cinematic videos that stand out and tell compelling visual stories.

The Motorola Razr 2024 Flip's camera system is more than just a feature—it's a gateway to exploring your creativity. With Pro Mode, advanced editing tools, versatile accessories, and cinematic video capabilities, the possibilities for capturing and creating are virtually limitless. Whether you're a casual photographer or an aspiring filmmaker, this chapter equips you with the knowledge and tools to take full advantage of the Razr's impressive camera features.

Entertainment and Streaming

The Motorola Razr 2024 Flip is not only a communication device but also a powerhouse for entertainment and streaming. Whether you're binge-watching your favorite TV shows, catching up on the latest movies, or managing multiple subscription services, the Razr is equipped to provide an exceptional entertainment experience. This chapter explores the best apps for watching content, how to optimize video quality for streaming, ways to use the external display for quick access, and effective management of your subscription services.

Best Apps for Watching Movies and Shows

The Google Play Store offers a vast array of apps designed to bring high-quality movies, TV shows, and live content directly to your Motorola Razr 2024 Flip. Selecting the right apps can transform your phone into a portable entertainment hub, offering endless viewing options tailored to your interests.

1. **Netflix**: Known for its extensive library of movies, TV series, and original content, Netflix is a must-have for entertainment enthusiasts. Its adaptive streaming ensures smooth playback even on variable networks.
2. **YouTube**: With millions of videos ranging from tutorials to live streams, YouTube is a versatile platform for all types of content. Its premium version eliminates ads and allows for offline downloads.
3. **Disney+**: Perfect for families, Disney+ offers a vast selection of Disney classics, Marvel films, Star Wars, and National Geographic documentaries.
4. **Amazon Prime Video**: This app provides a mix of popular movies, TV shows, and exclusive

originals. It also supports offline viewing for long commutes or travel.

5. **Hulu**: Known for its current TV episodes, Hulu combines on-demand streaming with live TV options, making it a versatile choice.

6. **HBO Max**: Ideal for those who love premium content, HBO Max includes blockbuster movies, critically acclaimed series, and an extensive catalog of Warner Bros. classics.

7. **Spotify and YouTube Music**: For music lovers, these apps offer high-quality streaming and curated playlists to keep you entertained between videos.

Installing these apps gives you access to a wide variety of content, from blockbuster hits to niche indie films, all tailored to your preferences.

Optimizing Video Quality for Streaming

The Motorola Razr 2024 Flip is equipped with a stunning pOLED display that enhances the viewing experience with vibrant colors, deep contrasts, and sharp resolutions. However, optimizing video quality is essential for maximizing your streaming experience, especially on different network conditions.

To optimize video quality:

1. **Adjust Streaming Settings in Apps**: Most streaming apps allow you to set the video quality based on your preferences. For example, in Netflix, go to **Settings > Playback Settings** and select **High** for the best quality. Keep in mind that higher quality consumes more data.

2. **Enable Adaptive Streaming**: Many apps, such as YouTube and Amazon Prime Video, offer adaptive streaming, which adjusts video quality automatically based on your network speed. This ensures smooth playback without buffering.

3. **Use Wi-Fi for High-Resolution Streaming**: Streaming in 1080p or 4K is best done over a stable Wi-Fi connection to avoid interruptions and excessive data usage.

4. **Activate Dolby Vision and HDR**: The Razr's display supports advanced video technologies like HDR10+ and Dolby Vision. Ensure these settings are enabled in apps that support them, such as Netflix and Disney+.

5. **Manage Brightness and Display Settings**: Watching videos in a well-lit environment may require higher brightness levels, while darker rooms can benefit from adaptive brightness. Access these options through **Settings > Display** to customize your viewing experience.

Optimizing video quality not only enhances your viewing experience but also ensures that you make the most of your device's display capabilities.

Using the External Display for Quick Access

One of the standout features of the Motorola Razr 2024 Flip is its functional external display, which allows you to interact with your phone without unfolding it. This feature is particularly useful for quick access to entertainment apps and media controls.

The external display supports widgets and shortcuts, enabling you to:

1. **Control Playback**: While streaming music or videos, the external display shows playback controls, allowing you to pause, skip, or rewind content without opening the phone.
2. **Preview Notifications**: Notifications from streaming apps like Netflix or YouTube appear on the external display, letting you know when new episodes or live streams are available.
3. **Launch Quick Widgets**: Add widgets for your favorite entertainment apps to the external display. For instance, a Spotify widget lets you browse playlists, and a YouTube widget provides shortcuts to trending videos.

4. **Stream on the Cover Screen**: Some apps allow you to watch videos directly on the external display. While this is ideal for quick previews or short clips, the main display is better suited for extended viewing sessions.

The external display adds an extra layer of convenience, making it easy to manage your entertainment on the go.

Managing Subscription Services

With so many streaming platforms available, managing subscriptions can become overwhelming. The Motorola Razr 2024 Flip simplifies this process with tools and apps that help you stay organized and avoid unnecessary charges.

1. **Track Subscriptions with Apps**: Use subscription management apps like Truebill or Bobby to monitor your active subscriptions. These apps provide a centralized view of all your services, including billing dates and costs.
2. **Consolidate Services**: Some platforms, like Amazon Prime Channels, allow you to bundle multiple streaming services under one account. This reduces the need for separate apps and simplifies billing.
3. **Set Reminders for Renewals**: Use the built-in calendar app to set reminders for subscription

renewals or free trial expirations. This ensures you don't forget to cancel services you no longer use.

4. **Monitor Usage**: Review your streaming habits to determine which services you use most frequently. Cancel subscriptions to platforms you rarely watch to save money.

5. **Leverage Family Plans**: Many streaming platforms, such as Netflix and Spotify, offer family plans that allow multiple users to share one subscription at a reduced cost.

Taking control of your subscriptions ensures that you enjoy your favorite content without overspending or juggling too many apps.

The Motorola Razr 2024 Flip is built for entertainment, offering tools and features that make streaming and managing content effortless. From discovering the best apps and optimizing video quality to leveraging the external display and managing subscriptions, this device is a gateway to an enhanced entertainment experience. Whether you're watching blockbuster movies, enjoying music, or catching up on your favorite shows, the Razr makes it all accessible, seamless, and enjoyable.

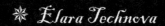

※ *Elara Technova*

Accessories for the Motorola Razr

The Motorola Razr 2024 Flip is a premium device that benefits from the right accessories to enhance its functionality, protection, and convenience. Whether you're looking to safeguard your phone, extend battery life, improve audio quality, or optimize your viewing experience, the right accessories can make all the difference. This chapter delves into essential accessories such as cases, screen protectors, chargers, power banks, wireless earbuds, headphones, and foldable phone stands, offering a comprehensive guide to choosing the best options for your device.

Cases and Screen Protectors

Protecting your Motorola Razr 2024 Flip is crucial to maintaining its pristine appearance and ensuring its longevity. As a foldable phone, it has unique design considerations that require specialized cases and screen protectors.

Cases for the Razr:

Foldable phones like the Razr require cases that offer protection without interfering with the hinge mechanism. Look for cases designed specifically for the Motorola Razr 2024 Flip, as they are engineered to fit snugly and accommodate the phone's folding design.

- **Hinge Covers**: Some cases include a hinge cover to protect this critical component from scratches and impacts.
- **Slim Profile Cases**: Slim cases provide basic protection while maintaining the sleek design of the Razr. They are lightweight and ideal for users who prefer minimal bulk.

- **Rugged Cases**: For those who prioritize durability, rugged cases offer enhanced drop protection, shock absorption, and grip. These cases are perfect for users who frequently handle their phones in demanding environments.
- **Clear Cases**: Clear cases showcase the Razr's elegant design while providing protection against scratches and minor impacts.

Screen Protectors for the Razr:

The foldable display and external screen on the Razr require specialized screen protectors that are flexible and durable.

- **Flexible Film Protectors**: These are made from ultra-thin materials that can bend with the screen. They are ideal for protecting the main foldable display without hindering its functionality.
- **Glass Protectors for the External Screen**: The external display can benefit from tempered glass protectors, which provide excellent scratch and impact resistance.

Applying a high-quality case and screen protector ensures that your phone stays safe from everyday wear and tear, helping you preserve its value over time.

The Motorola Razr 2024 Flip supports TurboPower charging, making it essential to choose chargers and power banks that complement this feature. Reliable power accessories ensure fast and efficient charging, whether you're at home, in the office, or on the go.

Chargers:

- **Motorola TurboPower Charger**: This official accessory delivers up to 30W of power, allowing you to charge your Razr quickly and efficiently. It's the best option for ensuring compatibility and optimal performance.
- **USB-C Chargers**: Third-party USB-C chargers that support Power Delivery (PD) are also suitable for the Razr. Look for models with at least 30W output for fast charging. Brands like Anker and Belkin offer high-quality options.

Power Banks:

- **Fast-Charging Power Banks**: Choose a power bank with Power Delivery support and a capacity of at least 10,000mAh to recharge your Razr multiple times. For heavy users, a 20,000mAh power bank provides even greater flexibility.

- **Compact Power Banks**: Slim and lightweight power banks are ideal for travel or daily commutes, offering a balance between portability and capacity.
- **Wireless Power Banks**: Some power banks feature wireless charging pads, allowing you to charge your Razr cable-free. Ensure the power bank is Qi-compatible for seamless operation.

Investing in reliable chargers and power banks ensures that your Razr stays powered throughout the day, even during intensive usage or long trips.

Best Wireless Earbuds and Headphones

The Motorola Razr 2024 Flip pairs perfectly with wireless earbuds and headphones, delivering an exceptional audio experience for calls, music, and media. With Bluetooth 5.4 compatibility, the Razr supports a wide range of wireless audio accessories.

Wireless Earbuds:

- **Motorola VerveBuds**: These earbuds are designed for seamless integration with Motorola devices, offering balanced sound, long battery life, and a comfortable fit.
- **Apple AirPods Pro**: Known for their active noise cancellation and excellent sound quality,

AirPods Pro work well with the Razr despite being an Apple product.

- **Samsung Galaxy Buds2 Pro**: These earbuds provide crystal-clear audio, a comfortable fit, and support for high-resolution sound.
- **Jabra Elite 7 Pro**: Ideal for professionals, these earbuds feature advanced noise-canceling technology and excellent call quality.

Wireless Headphones:

- **Sony WH-1000XM5**: These industry-leading headphones offer superior noise cancellation, rich sound, and comfortable over-ear design, making them ideal for immersive media experiences.
- **Bose QuietComfort 45**: Known for their comfort and balanced audio, these headphones are a great choice for long listening sessions.
- **Sennheiser Momentum 4 Wireless**: These headphones deliver premium sound quality and a modern design, perfect for audiophiles.

Choose earbuds or headphones based on your preferences for sound quality, comfort, and features like active noise cancellation or water resistance.

Foldable phone stands enhance the usability of the Motorola Razr 2024 Flip, allowing you to enjoy hands-free viewing and multitasking. These accessories are especially useful for watching videos, participating in video calls, or using the phone in Flex View mode.

Types of Foldable Phone Stands:

- **Adjustable Stands**: These stands let you change the viewing angle, making them versatile for different activities. Look for models with sturdy construction and non-slip bases.
- **Portable Stands**: Compact and lightweight stands are easy to carry, making them perfect for travel or on-the-go use.
- **Multi-Purpose Stands**: Some stands double as phone holders for cars or as charging docks, providing added functionality.
- **Magnetic Stands**: Magnetic stands offer quick and secure mounting for your phone, ideal for desk setups or kitchen use.

When selecting a stand, ensure it supports the Razr's folding design and provides a stable base for both landscape and portrait orientations.

Accessories for the Motorola Razr 2024 Flip enhance its functionality, protect its unique design, and elevate your overall user experience. By investing in high-quality cases, chargers, audio devices, and stands, you can make the most of your foldable smartphone while ensuring it remains in excellent condition. Whether you prioritize style, convenience, or durability, these accessories cater to every need and preference.

Advanced Features for Power Users

The Motorola Razr 2024 Flip is not just a device for everyday use; it's also packed with advanced features designed for power users who want to unlock its full potential. Whether you're a developer, gamer, or simply a tech enthusiast, the Razr offers tools and settings that enhance customization, functionality, and performance. In this chapter, we will explore enabling developer options, using USB debugging, discovering hidden features, and configuring advanced settings for gamers.

Enabling Developer Options

Developer Options is a hidden menu in Android that provides access to a variety of advanced settings and tools. These options are invaluable for power users who want to customize their phone, test applications, or optimize performance.

To enable Developer Options on your Motorola Razr 2024 Flip:

1. Open the **Settings** app and navigate to **About Phone**.
2. Scroll down to **Build Number** and tap it seven times. You'll see a notification that says, "You are now a developer!"
3. Go back to the **Settings** menu, and you'll find **Developer Options** under the **System** section.

Once enabled, Developer Options unlocks a range of features, such as animation scaling, debugging tools, and hardware acceleration settings. These options give you greater control over how your device operates, allowing for deeper customization and enhanced functionality.

USB Debugging is one of the most important features within Developer Options. It allows your phone to communicate with a computer for tasks like transferring data, installing apps, or testing software. This feature is particularly useful for developers and those who want to sideload apps or perform advanced troubleshooting.

To enable USB Debugging:

1. Go to **Settings > System > Developer Options**.
2. Scroll down to **USB Debugging** and toggle it on.
3. Connect your phone to a computer using a USB-C cable. You'll see a prompt on your phone asking for permission to allow USB debugging. Tap **Allow**.

USB Debugging can be used for several purposes:

- **App Testing**: Developers can test their applications directly on the Razr by connecting it to Android Studio or other development tools.
- **File Transfers**: Access your phone's internal storage from a computer to transfer files or back up important data.

- **Sideloading Apps**: Install apps that aren't available on the Google Play Store by transferring APK files to your device.
- **Command Line Operations**: Use ADB (Android Debug Bridge) commands to perform advanced tasks, such as unlocking the bootloader, capturing screenshots, or managing app data.

While USB Debugging is a powerful tool, it's important to disable it when not in use to prevent unauthorized access to your phone.

Exploring Hidden Features

The Motorola Razr 2024 Flip includes several hidden features that enhance its usability and provide additional functionality. These features are often overlooked but can significantly improve your experience.

- **Gestures and Shortcuts**: The Razr supports intuitive gestures like the double twist to quickly launch the camera or the chop motion to turn on the flashlight. Enable these gestures in **Settings > Gestures** for faster access to frequently used features.
- **Split-Screen Multitasking**: Use two apps simultaneously with the split-screen feature. Open an app, then tap the **Recent Apps** button and select **Split Screen**. This is perfect for

multitasking, such as watching a video while replying to messages.

- **Smart Lock**: Smart Lock keeps your phone unlocked in trusted environments, such as when it's connected to a specific Bluetooth device or when you're at home. Access this feature in **Settings > Security > Smart Lock**.
- **App Pinning**: Pin an app to the screen to prevent others from accessing your phone's other functions. This is useful when lending your phone to someone for a specific task. Enable it in **Settings > Security > Advanced > App Pinning**.
- **Scheduled Power On/Off**: Automate when your phone powers on or off to save battery and reduce interruptions. Configure this in **Settings > System > Scheduled Power On/Off**.

These hidden features are designed to make your device more convenient and efficient, whether for everyday tasks or advanced use.

Advanced Settings for Gamers

Gamers will appreciate the Motorola Razr 2024 Flip's ability to deliver smooth and immersive gaming experiences. With features like high refresh rate support, customizable graphics settings, and game mode optimizations, the Razr is built to handle demanding mobile games.

- **Game Time Mode**: Access Game Time mode from **Settings > Gaming Tools**. This feature enhances gaming performance by blocking notifications, freeing up system resources, and optimizing battery usage. You can also use the Game Dashboard to record gameplay, take screenshots, or access shortcuts without leaving the game.
- **Graphics Optimization**: Many games allow you to customize graphics settings, such as resolution, frame rate, and texture quality. Use these settings to balance performance and visual quality based on your preferences. The Razr's high refresh rate display ensures smooth gameplay, especially in fast-paced games like shooters or racing titles.
- **Customize Touch Sensitivity**: For games that require precision, adjust the touch sensitivity settings in **Settings > Display > Touch Sensitivity**. This ensures responsive controls, even when using a screen protector.
- **Pair with Gaming Accessories**: Enhance your gaming experience by connecting Bluetooth controllers, such as the Xbox or PlayStation controller, for console-like gameplay. Additionally, consider using a foldable phone stand to prop the Razr in Flex View mode for hands-free gaming.
- **Monitor Performance**: Use third-party apps like Game Booster to monitor your phone's CPU,

GPU, and temperature during gaming sessions. These tools help you identify any performance bottlenecks and make necessary adjustments.

With these advanced settings, the Motorola Razr 2024 Flip transforms into a gaming powerhouse, offering smooth and responsive gameplay for both casual and competitive gamers.

The advanced features of the Motorola Razr 2024 Flip cater to power users who want more control and functionality from their device. From enabling Developer Options and USB Debugging to exploring hidden features and optimizing settings for gaming, this chapter provides a comprehensive guide to unlocking the full potential of your Razr. With these tools at your disposal, you can customize and optimize your phone to suit your specific needs and preferences.

Using the External Display

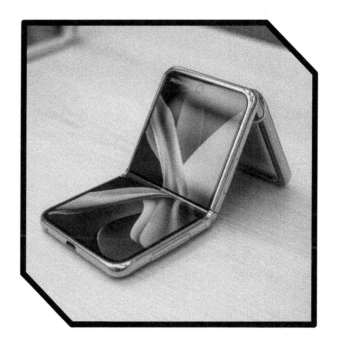

The external display on the Motorola Razr 2024 Flip is more than just a secondary screen—it's a highly functional tool that enhances convenience and productivity. This compact display provides quick access to essential features, making it an integral part of the Razr's design. Whether you want to customize controls, manage notifications, boost productivity, or take photos without unfolding the phone, the external display offers incredible versatility. This chapter explains how to set up quick controls, customize notifications and widgets, maximize productivity, and use the external display for photography.

Setting Up Quick Controls

The external display is designed for instant access to key functions, allowing you to perform tasks quickly and efficiently without opening the phone. Setting up quick controls ensures that your most-used features are readily available with minimal effort.

To set up quick controls:

1. **Access the Settings Menu**: Go to **Settings > External Display** to configure the available options.
2. **Enable Quick Settings**: Customize the Quick Settings panel to include essential controls such as Wi-Fi, Bluetooth, Do Not Disturb, and Brightness Adjustment. Swipe down on the external display to access these settings instantly.
3. **Shortcuts for Frequently Used Apps**: Add shortcuts for your favorite apps like Music, Messages, or Camera. These can be accessed with a simple tap, saving time and effort.

4. **Gesture Controls**: The external display supports gestures for navigation. For instance, swipe left or right to toggle between widgets or notifications and swipe down for quick settings.

With these quick controls in place, you can manage your phone efficiently even when it's folded, making the external display a practical tool for everyday use.

Customizing Notifications and Widgets

Customizing notifications and widgets on the external display allows you to tailor the experience to suit your needs. The compact screen can show real-time updates, manage alerts, and provide at-a-glance information, keeping you informed without distractions.

Customizing Notifications:

1. **Notification Settings**: Go to **Settings > Notifications** and enable specific apps for the external display. Choose which apps can send alerts to avoid being overwhelmed by unnecessary notifications.
2. **Grouped Notifications**: The external display can group notifications by app, allowing you to view updates from similar sources in one place. This helps keep your screen organized.

3. **Interactive Notifications**: Respond to messages, emails, or alerts directly from the external display using quick actions like reply, archive, or delete.

Adding and Customizing Widgets:

1. **Widget Selection**: In **Settings > External Display**, choose widgets for essential features like weather, calendar, fitness tracking, or music controls.
2. **Rearranging Widgets**: Drag and drop widgets to reorder them based on priority. Place your most-used widgets at the top for easy access.
3. **Personalized Themes**: Customize the external display's theme to match your style. Choose from various backgrounds, colors, and font styles to make the screen visually appealing.

By tailoring notifications and widgets, you can create a streamlined and intuitive interface that delivers relevant information at a glance.

Maximizing Productivity with the Cover Screen

The external display isn't just for convenience; it's a powerful productivity tool that helps you stay organized and efficient. With its ability to handle tasks without unfolding the phone, the cover screen minimizes distractions and saves time.

Tips for Boosting Productivity:

1. **Calendar and Reminders**: Use the calendar widget to view upcoming events or set reminders for important tasks. The external display allows you to check your schedule quickly without interrupting your workflow.
2. **Voice Commands**: Activate Google Assistant on the external display for hands-free productivity. Use voice commands to send messages, set alarms, or search the web.
3. **Media Controls**: Control your music or podcasts directly from the external display. Pause, skip, or adjust the volume without navigating through multiple menus.
4. **Multitasking**: The external display supports quick replies to messages, enabling you to communicate while focusing on other tasks.
5. **Time Management**: Add a clock widget with world time zones if you collaborate with teams in different locations. This helps you schedule meetings effectively.

The external display's productivity features make it a valuable asset for professionals, students, and anyone looking to manage their time more effectively.

One of the standout features of the external display is its ability to function as a viewfinder for the Razr's camera. This is particularly useful for quick photography, allowing you to capture high-quality photos without unfolding the device.

Using the External Display for Photos:

1. **Launch the Camera**: Double-press the power button or tap the camera shortcut on the external display to open the camera instantly.

2. **Selfies Made Easy**: Use the external display as a viewfinder for selfies. The Razr's rear camera provides superior quality compared to the front-facing camera, ensuring sharper and more detailed photos.

3. **Portrait and Group Shots**: The external display allows you to frame your shots accurately, making it ideal for group photos or portraits. Use the countdown timer for hands-free captures.

4. **Gesture Controls**: The Razr supports gestures like showing your palm to start a countdown for selfies, making the process even more seamless.

5. **Preview and Edit**: Review your photos on the external display and make basic adjustments like cropping or deleting right from the screen.

The ability to use the external display for quick photography not only enhances convenience but also ensures that you're always ready to capture the perfect moment.

The Motorola Razr 2024 Flip's external display is a versatile feature that goes beyond aesthetics. From setting up quick controls and customizing notifications to maximizing productivity and capturing high-quality photos, the external display adds significant value to the overall user experience. It's a tool that combines functionality and convenience, making your smartphone even more efficient and enjoyable to use.

Business and Professional Use

The Motorola Razr 2024 Flip is not only a stylish and innovative smartphone but also a powerful tool for business and professional use. Its advanced features, sleek design, and productivity-focused capabilities make it an excellent choice for professionals who need to stay organized and connected. This chapter explores how to sync with work apps, effectively use cloud

166

storage, manage documents, and host video calls seamlessly. These features allow users to optimize their professional tasks while maintaining convenience and efficiency.

Syncing with Work Apps

One of the key strengths of the Motorola Razr 2024 Flip is its ability to integrate seamlessly with a wide range of work apps, helping you stay connected and productive. Syncing your Razr with essential business tools ensures that you can manage tasks, collaborate with colleagues, and access important information on the go.

To get started, download the work apps you use regularly, such as Microsoft Teams, Slack, Zoom, Google Workspace (Gmail, Calendar, Drive), or Microsoft Office Suite, from the Google Play Store. Once installed, sign in using your work credentials to sync your accounts. Enable notifications for these apps so you never miss important updates or messages.

The Razr's split-screen mode is particularly useful for multitasking. For instance, you can attend a Zoom meeting on one half of the screen while taking notes in Google Docs on the other. The phone's high-resolution display ensures that text and visuals are crisp, even when multitasking.

Syncing with your company's email and calendar apps ensures that you stay on top of meetings, deadlines, and tasks, keeping your workflow smooth and organized.

Using Cloud Storage Effectively

Cloud storage is a vital tool for professionals, offering secure access to files from anywhere. The Motorola Razr 2024 Flip supports a variety of cloud storage services, including Google Drive, Dropbox, OneDrive, and Box, making it easy to store, share, and manage documents.

To use cloud storage effectively, start by linking your preferred cloud service to the phone. For example, if you use Google Drive, sign in with your Google account and enable automatic backups for important files. You can upload documents, spreadsheets, presentations, and even media files directly to the cloud, ensuring that they are safe and accessible whenever you need them.

The Razr's external display adds an extra layer of convenience. For quick access to files, you can preview recent uploads or download important documents directly from the cover screen. Sharing files is also simple. Whether you're sending large presentations to colleagues or collaborating on shared folders, the cloud storage apps make the process seamless.

Additionally, cloud storage reduces the risk of losing important data due to hardware issues. Regularly back up your files to the cloud to ensure that your work remains secure, even if your device is damaged or lost. This feature is especially beneficial for professionals who frequently travel or work remotely.

Managing Documents on the Razr

Managing documents on the Motorola Razr 2024 Flip is both easy and efficient. The phone's high-performance hardware and user-friendly interface make it a versatile tool for handling a wide range of document types, including PDFs, Word files, Excel sheets, and presentations.

To get started, install document management apps like Adobe Acrobat, Microsoft Office, or Google Docs. These apps allow you to view, edit, and share documents directly from your device. For example, Adobe Acrobat is ideal for reviewing and annotating PDFs, while Microsoft Word and Google Docs provide robust editing tools for creating or updating text-based documents.

The Razr's foldable display enhances productivity by providing a larger workspace for editing and reviewing documents. You can use split-screen mode to compare two files side by side or collaborate on a document while communicating with team members via a messaging app. The device's responsive touch controls and smooth scrolling make it easy to navigate lengthy documents without hassle.

For organizing your files, use the built-in file manager or a third-party app like Solid Explorer. Create folders for different projects, clients, or categories to keep your files organized and easily accessible. Pair this with cloud storage to ensure that all your documents are synchronized and available across devices.

The external display also offers quick document management capabilities. For instance, you can preview emails with attachments, forward files, or respond to urgent edits directly from the cover screen without needing to unfold the phone. This feature is particularly helpful during meetings or when you're on the move.

Hosting Video Calls

Video calls are an essential part of modern business communication, and the Motorola Razr 2024 Flip excels in this area with its high-quality cameras, robust performance, and reliable connectivity. Whether you're hosting a team meeting, attending a client presentation, or collaborating with remote colleagues, the Razr ensures a smooth and professional video call experience.

To host video calls, install popular apps like Zoom, Microsoft Teams, or Google Meet. The Razr's foldable design allows you to set up the phone in Flex View mode, turning it into a hands-free video conferencing tool. Simply fold the phone halfway and place it on a flat surface to create a stable stand. This eliminates the need for additional accessories and keeps your hands free for note-taking or multitasking.

The phone's external display provides a preview of incoming video calls, allowing you to quickly join meetings without fully opening the device. Once in a call, the Razr's dual microphones and noise cancellation technology ensure clear audio, while the high-resolution camera delivers sharp visuals.

For group calls, the phone's wide-angle camera captures more of the scene, making it ideal for team discussions. Use the built-in camera settings to adjust brightness, focus, and filters for the best appearance during calls.

To enhance the experience further, connect wireless earbuds or headphones for better audio clarity and privacy. If you're working on a collaborative project, screen sharing features in apps like Zoom and Teams allow you to present documents, slides, or designs directly from your Razr.

Hosting video calls on the Razr is seamless, professional, and convenient, making it a valuable tool for professionals who rely on virtual meetings for collaboration and communication.

The Motorola Razr 2024 Flip is a versatile companion for business and professional use, offering powerful tools to manage work apps, documents, cloud storage, and video calls. With its advanced features and user-friendly design, it ensures that professionals can stay productive, organized, and connected, no matter where they are.

Integrating Motorola Apps

Motorola has built a strong ecosystem of apps and tools designed to enhance the user experience, optimize productivity, and seamlessly connect your Motorola Razr 2024 Flip with other devices. These apps are tailored to meet the needs of a modern, tech-savvy audience, providing both functionality and convenience. This chapter explores the introduction to Motorola Ready

For, a deep dive into exclusive Motorola tools, the benefits of Motorola's ecosystem, and potential future updates for its apps.

Introduction to Motorola Ready For

Motorola Ready For is a standout feature that transforms your Razr into a versatile hub for work, play, and communication. This platform allows you to connect your Razr to a larger screen, such as a TV or monitor, enabling you to use your phone like a desktop computer. Ready For bridges the gap between mobile and desktop functionality, making it a powerful tool for multitasking and enhanced productivity.

Setting up Motorola Ready For is simple. All you need is a USB-C to HDMI cable or a wireless connection for compatible devices. Once connected, your phone's interface adjusts to provide a desktop-like experience. You can open multiple apps in separate windows, drag and drop files, and even use the Razr as a touchpad or keyboard. This feature is particularly useful for creating presentations, editing documents, or streaming content on a larger screen.

In addition to productivity, Motorola Ready For enhances entertainment and communication. You can enjoy immersive gaming on a big screen, use video chat apps with the Razr's high-quality cameras, or mirror your phone's content to share photos and videos with family and friends. Ready For also supports peripherals like Bluetooth keyboards and mice, further enhancing its desktop functionality.

Exploring Exclusive Motorola Tools

Motorola has developed a range of exclusive tools that are designed to improve the usability and versatility of the Razr. These tools cater to various aspects of user needs, from customization and security to enhanced media controls.

1. **Moto Actions**: Moto Actions offers gesture-based controls that simplify everyday tasks. For instance, you can chop twice to turn on the flashlight, twist your wrist to open the camera, or flip the phone face down to enable Do Not Disturb mode. These intuitive gestures make interacting with your phone faster and more convenient.

2. **Moto Display**: This feature provides a glanceable view of notifications and updates without fully waking the screen. The Razr's external display takes this a step further by showing detailed previews of messages, calls, and app notifications. Moto Display also allows for quick interactions, such as

replying to messages or dismissing notifications directly from the cover screen.

3. **Gametime Mode**: For gamers, Gametime Mode optimizes your phone's performance during gameplay by blocking notifications, prioritizing resources, and providing a streamlined gaming interface. You can also record gameplay or take screenshots without interruptions.

4. **Ready For Mobile Desktop**: This tool complements Motorola Ready For by enabling a desktop-like interface directly on your phone. It's perfect for on-the-go productivity, allowing you to work on tasks such as email management or spreadsheet editing with ease.

These tools are pre-installed on the Razr, ensuring that users have access to advanced features right out of the box. They are designed to enhance usability while maintaining the phone's sleek and intuitive interface.

Benefits of Motorola's Ecosystem

The Motorola ecosystem is designed to create a seamless and interconnected experience for its users. By integrating Motorola apps and tools with the Razr 2024 Flip, you can unlock a wide range of benefits that make the phone more versatile and efficient.

One of the key advantages is **cross-device compatibility**. Motorola Ready For allows you to connect your Razr to monitors, TVs, and laptops, creating a unified workspace. This eliminates the need for multiple devices and enables you to switch between tasks effortlessly. For example, you can start editing a document on your phone and continue working on it on a larger screen without losing your progress.

Another benefit is **enhanced productivity**. Motorola's apps, such as Moto Actions and Moto Display, streamline everyday tasks, saving time and effort. Features like one-touch replies, intuitive gestures, and multitasking capabilities ensure that you can stay productive throughout the day.

The ecosystem also prioritizes **security and privacy**. Motorola's apps include robust security measures, such as encryption and secure folder options, to protect your data. You can use features like biometric authentication (fingerprint or face unlock) to safeguard sensitive information.

Lastly, the Motorola ecosystem is designed to be **user-friendly and accessible**. The apps are intuitive, requiring minimal setup or technical knowledge. This ensures that users of all skill levels can take advantage of the phone's advanced features without feeling overwhelmed.

Future Updates for Motorola Apps

Motorola is committed to innovation, and its apps are regularly updated to introduce new features, enhance performance, and improve user experience. The future of Motorola's ecosystem is likely to include several advancements, making the Razr 2024 Flip an even more powerful device.

One area of focus is **AI-powered enhancements**. Future updates may include smarter notifications, where the phone learns your preferences and prioritizes important alerts. AI could also be used to optimize performance by predicting and preloading frequently used apps.

Another potential update is **deeper integration with third-party apps and services**. For instance, Motorola Ready For could expand its compatibility with more peripherals, streaming platforms, and productivity tools. This would make the platform even more versatile for both work and entertainment.

Motorola is also likely to enhance **security features**, addressing growing concerns about data privacy. Future updates may include advanced encryption methods, improved biometric authentication, and more robust protection against malware and phishing attacks.

Finally, Motorola is expected to continue improving **user customization options**. This could include additional themes, widgets, and gesture controls that allow users to tailor their phones to their specific needs. Updates to Moto Actions and Moto Display could introduce new gestures or functionalities, further enhancing the user experience.

The Motorola Razr 2024 Flip's integration with Motorola apps provides users with an ecosystem that is both functional and innovative. From the versatile capabilities of Motorola Ready For to the user-friendly tools like Moto Actions and Moto Display, these apps enhance the phone's usability and performance. With regular updates and a focus on seamless connectivity, Motorola's ecosystem ensures that the Razr remains at the forefront of mobile technology, delivering value and convenience for every user.

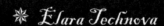

Photography for Social Media

The Motorola Razr 2024 Flip is more than just a smartphone—it's a versatile tool for creating high-quality content tailored for social media platforms. With its advanced camera system, foldable design, and powerful software, the Razr is perfect for capturing Instagram-worthy photos, shooting engaging TikTok or Reels videos, and editing content that stands out. This chapter focuses on how to create content for social media, from capturing stunning photos to editing and sharing them seamlessly across platforms.

Creating Instagram-Ready Photos

Instagram is a visual platform where the quality and creativity of your photos matter most. The Motorola Razr 2024 Flip's camera system, featuring a high-resolution main lens and advanced photo modes, ensures that your photos are crisp, vibrant, and ready to wow your audience.

To create Instagram-ready photos, start by exploring the camera's **Portrait Mode**, which blurs the background for professional-looking shots. This feature is ideal for selfies, fashion photos, or any subject where you want to draw attention to the foreground. Use **HDR (High Dynamic Range)** to capture well-balanced images in scenes with bright and dark areas, such as sunsets or cityscapes.

Lighting plays a critical role in photography, and the Razr's Night Vision feature ensures your photos look great even in low-light settings. Whether you're capturing a candlelit dinner or an evening skyline, Night Vision brings out the details and colors without noise.

Composition is another key element. Use the **gridlines** feature in the camera settings to apply the rule of thirds, which helps you frame your shots for better visual appeal. For added creativity, experiment with angles. The Razr's foldable design lets you position the phone at unique angles, making it easy to take low or high shots hands-free.

Finally, adjust the **aspect ratio** to fit Instagram's preferred formats. Square (1:1) and portrait (4:5) ratios work best for posts, while 16:9 is great for stories. You can adjust these settings directly in the camera app to save time during editing.

Shooting TikTok and Reels Videos

TikTok and Instagram Reels thrive on engaging, creative, and fast-paced video content. The Motorola Razr 2024 Flip makes it easy to shoot dynamic videos that grab attention and keep your audience entertained.

To start, use the Razr's **Flex View Mode**, which allows you to fold the phone and place it on a flat surface for hands-free recording. This is especially useful for dance videos, tutorials, or any scenario where you need to move freely. The phone's high refresh rate and advanced stabilization ensure that your videos are smooth and free of shakes.

When shooting videos, take advantage of the **Slow Motion** and **Time-Lapse** modes to add variety to your content. Slow Motion is perfect for dramatic effects, such as capturing hair flips or water splashes, while Time-Lapse works well for speeding up scenes like sunsets or city traffic.

Lighting is crucial for video content, so use a ring light or natural light whenever possible. The Razr's **Auto HDR** feature ensures balanced exposure, so your videos look great even in challenging lighting conditions. Experiment with different angles and perspectives to make your videos more visually appealing.

Audio is equally important for TikTok and Reels. The Razr's dual microphones provide clear sound quality, but you can also use an external microphone for professional-grade audio. Pair your videos with trending music or sound effects directly within the TikTok or Instagram app to increase their reach and engagement.

Using Editing Apps for Social Content

Editing is an essential step in creating polished, professional-looking content for social media. While the Motorola Razr 2024 Flip offers built-in editing tools, using third-party apps can provide additional features and creative options.

For photo editing, apps like **Adobe Lightroom**, **Snapseed**, and **VSCO** are excellent choices. These apps allow you to adjust brightness, contrast, saturation, and sharpness with precision. You can also apply filters to give your photos a consistent aesthetic that aligns with your social media theme. For example, warm tones work well for lifestyle accounts, while vibrant colors are great for travel photography.

For video editing, apps like **CapCut**, **InShot**, and **Adobe Premiere Rush** are highly recommended. These tools let you trim clips, add transitions, insert text overlays, and adjust playback speed. You can also add music, sound effects, and stickers to make your videos more engaging.

When editing, keep the platform in mind. Instagram Reels and TikTok favor vertical videos, so crop your footage to a 9:16 aspect ratio. Optimize the resolution and frame rate to ensure your content looks sharp on mobile devices.

If you're managing a cohesive brand or personal aesthetic, consider using **preset filters** or creating a unique style for your content. This helps build a recognizable visual identity that sets your profile apart from others.

Sharing content seamlessly across platforms is crucial for maintaining an active and engaging social media presence. The Motorola Razr 2024 Flip simplifies this process with its powerful sharing tools and intuitive interface.

Start by organizing your photos and videos in folders or albums within the phone's gallery app. This makes it easier to locate the content you want to post. Use the Razr's **quick sharing options**, which allow you to send content directly to Instagram, TikTok, or other apps with just a tap.

Before posting, use the **Preview** feature in social media apps to ensure your content appears exactly how you want it. For example, check that captions, hashtags, and tags are correctly formatted. The Razr's external display provides a quick way to review notifications and respond to comments without interrupting your workflow.

To save time, use scheduling tools like **Later**, **Hootsuite**, or **Meta Business Suite** to plan and schedule your posts in advance. These tools let you upload content, write captions, and select posting times, ensuring a consistent presence on social media.

For collaborative projects or campaigns, share your content with teammates or clients using cloud services like Google Drive or Dropbox. These platforms make it easy to transfer large files while maintaining their quality.

The Motorola Razr 2024 Flip is a powerful companion for social media enthusiasts and content creators. From capturing Instagram-ready photos to shooting dynamic TikTok videos, editing content like a pro, and sharing seamlessly across platforms, this phone is equipped with everything you need to shine online. With its advanced camera features, versatile design, and user-friendly tools, the Razr enables you to create stunning content that captures attention and grows your audience.

Practical Tips for Everyday Use

The Motorola Razr 2024 Flip is designed to seamlessly integrate into your daily life, offering features that enhance convenience and efficiency. However, like any advanced device, using it effectively requires adopting a few practical tips and habits. This chapter provides detailed guidance on the best shortcuts for daily tasks, managing storage space efficiently, maintaining the longevity of the foldable parts, and helpful habits for smooth operation. These tips will help you make the most of your device while ensuring it remains in excellent condition.

Best Shortcuts for Daily Tasks

The Motorola Razr 2024 Flip is packed with shortcuts and gestures that simplify daily tasks and save time. These features are designed to make common actions more intuitive, reducing the number of steps required to complete them.

- **Quick Launch for Apps**: Use the external display to access frequently used apps without opening the phone. You can customize the shortcuts menu in the settings, adding apps like Camera, Messages, or Music for one-tap access.
- **Moto Actions**: Motorola's Moto Actions feature offers gesture-based shortcuts that are incredibly handy for daily use. For instance, you can twist your wrist twice to open the camera instantly or chop the phone twice to turn on the flashlight. These simple gestures make it easy to perform essential actions in seconds.
- **One-Handed Mode**: Activate one-handed mode to make navigating the phone more comfortable when you're multitasking or holding something in your other hand. This

feature adjusts the screen display to make it easier to reach all areas with one thumb.

- **Voice Commands**: Enable Google Assistant for hands-free operation. Use voice commands to send messages, set alarms, play music, or get directions without touching your phone.
- **Quick Settings Toggles**: Customize the quick settings panel to include your most-used functions, such as Wi-Fi, Bluetooth, and screen brightness. Swipe down on the main or external display to access these settings quickly.

These shortcuts not only improve efficiency but also enhance the overall user experience by reducing repetitive actions and making navigation seamless.

Managing Storage Space Effectively

With its high-performance capabilities, the Motorola Razr 2024 Flip can quickly fill up with apps, photos, videos, and other data. Managing storage space effectively ensures that your device runs smoothly and has room for what matters most.

- **Review and Delete Unnecessary Files**: Regularly go through your photo gallery, downloads, and app cache to delete unnecessary files. Use the built-in file manager or third-party apps like

Files by Google to identify large files or duplicate items taking up space.

- **Use Cloud Storage**: Services like Google Drive, Dropbox, and OneDrive are excellent for offloading photos, videos, and documents. Enable automatic backups for your media files to free up local storage while keeping your data accessible.
- **Uninstall Unused Apps**: Periodically review the apps on your device and uninstall those you no longer use. Go to **Settings > Apps** to see a list of installed apps and their storage usage.
- **Move Apps to External Storage**: If your Razr supports expandable storage via microSD, move compatible apps and files to the SD card to save space on the internal storage.
- **Optimize Media Settings**: Adjust your camera settings to capture photos and videos in slightly lower resolutions if high-quality files are not necessary. For example, 1080p video takes up less space than 4K but still offers excellent quality for everyday use.

Effective storage management ensures that your Razr runs efficiently and has enough space for new apps, updates, and media files.

The foldable design of the Motorola Razr 2024 Flip is one of its most innovative features, but it requires special care to ensure its longevity. By following a few simple practices, you can maintain the durability and functionality of the hinge and foldable display.

- **Avoid Excessive Pressure**: Be gentle when opening and closing the phone. Avoid applying excessive pressure on the hinge or foldable display, as this can cause wear over time. Use a smooth, deliberate motion when folding or unfolding the device.
- **Keep the Hinge Clean**: Dust and debris can accumulate in the hinge mechanism, potentially affecting its performance. Regularly clean the hinge area with a soft brush or compressed air to keep it free of particles.
- **Use a Screen Protector**: Invest in a high-quality screen protector designed specifically for foldable displays. This adds an extra layer of protection against scratches and minor impacts without affecting the screen's flexibility.
- **Avoid Sharp Objects**: Keep the foldable screen away from sharp objects like keys, pens, or coins, as the flexible material is more susceptible to damage compared to traditional glass screens.

- **Store Safely**: When not in use, store your phone in a protective case that's designed for foldable devices. This ensures that the hinge and display remain protected from accidental bumps or falls.

By adopting these care practices, you can extend the lifespan of your Razr's foldable components and maintain its sleek, functional design.

Helpful Habits for Smooth Operation

Adopting good habits ensures that your Motorola Razr 2024 Flip operates smoothly and efficiently over time. These habits not only improve performance but also enhance your overall experience with the device.

- **Restart Regularly**: Restart your phone at least once a week to clear temporary files, refresh the system, and improve performance.
- **Update Software**: Keep your phone's operating system and apps up to date by enabling automatic updates. Software updates often include performance improvements, bug fixes, and new features.
- **Monitor Battery Health**: Use the built-in battery settings to track usage and identify apps that consume excessive power. Avoid letting

your battery drop below 20% or stay at 100% for prolonged periods to maintain its health.

- **Enable Adaptive Brightness**: Adaptive brightness adjusts the screen's brightness based on your surroundings, reducing eye strain and conserving battery life.
- **Use a Reliable Case and Screen Protector**: Invest in accessories that provide both protection and functionality. A good case and screen protector can prevent damage and keep your phone looking new.
- **Backup Your Data**: Enable automatic backups for your contacts, photos, and important files. This ensures that your data is secure and can be restored easily in case of accidental deletion or hardware failure.

Incorporating these habits into your daily routine will help you maintain your device's performance, extend its lifespan, and enjoy a hassle-free experience.

The Motorola Razr 2024 Flip is a cutting-edge device that can seamlessly adapt to your lifestyle with the right practices and habits. From shortcuts that streamline your daily tasks to maintenance tips that protect its foldable design, these practical tips ensure that your Razr remains efficient, reliable, and enjoyable to use in every aspect of your daily life.

Comparing the Motorola Razr to Competitors

The Motorola Razr 2024 Flip is a bold statement in the world of foldable smartphones, offering a unique combination of style, innovation, and functionality. In a competitive market filled with foldable devices, understanding how the Razr stacks up against its rivals can help highlight its strengths and unique appeal. This chapter provides an in-depth comparison of the Razr against Samsung's foldables, explores features exclusive to Motorola, examines the advantages of its build quality, and explains why the Razr 2024 Flip stands out as a game-changer in the industry.

How the Razr Stacks Up Against Samsung Foldables

Samsung's foldable lineup, particularly the Galaxy Z Flip series, has been a dominant player in the foldable smartphone market. However, the Motorola Razr 2024 Flip brings its own set of features and design elements that make it a worthy competitor.

One of the key differences between the Razr and Samsung's Z Flip models is the external display. The Razr 2024 Flip features a larger and more functional cover screen, which allows users to perform a wide range of tasks without opening the phone. From replying to messages and checking notifications to using widgets and running apps, the external display on the Razr offers a level of convenience that Samsung's smaller cover screen cannot match.

In terms of design, the Razr stands out with its sleek and nostalgic appeal, reminiscent of the iconic Razr flip phones of the past. While the Galaxy Z Flip leans towards a more modern aesthetic, the Razr combines retro charm with cutting-edge technology, making it a stylish choice for users who value both form and function.

When it comes to camera performance, the Razr 2024 Flip holds its own with advanced features like Night Vision, Pro Mode, and ultra-wide-angle capabilities. While Samsung foldables may offer higher megapixel counts in some models, the Razr's software optimization ensures excellent image quality in various lighting conditions.

Battery life and charging speeds are also areas where the Razr competes effectively. The inclusion of TurboPower charging ensures quick and efficient recharging, while the device's software optimizations help extend battery life during everyday use. Overall, the Razr offers a well-rounded package that rivals Samsung's foldables while providing unique advantages.

Unique Features Exclusive to the Razr

The Motorola Razr 2024 Flip sets itself apart from competitors with features that are exclusive to the Razr lineup. These unique elements enhance the overall user experience and provide added value for those who choose Motorola's foldable.

One standout feature is **Flex View Mode**, which allows the phone to be partially folded and placed on a surface for hands-free use. Whether you're on a video call, watching content, or taking selfies, Flex View Mode transforms the Razr into a versatile device that adapts to your needs.

The external display on the Razr is another exclusive highlight. Unlike competitors, the Razr's cover screen supports full app functionality, meaning you can run apps like Instagram, Spotify, or Google Maps without opening the phone. This level of interactivity is unmatched, making the external display a true extension of the device rather than a secondary screen.

Motorola's **Ready For** platform is yet another unique offering. This feature enables the Razr to connect seamlessly to TVs, monitors, and PCs, allowing users to enjoy a desktop-like experience. Whether you're working on documents, streaming content, or gaming, Ready For expands the Razr's capabilities far beyond what most foldable phones offer.

Finally, the Razr's nostalgic design, inspired by the original Razr flip phone, appeals to users who value a blend of modern technology and classic style.

This timeless design sets it apart from competitors that focus solely on futuristic aesthetics.

Advantages of Motorola's Build Quality

Motorola has long been recognized for its commitment to build quality, and the Razr 2024 Flip is no exception. The device is constructed with premium materials that ensure durability while maintaining a lightweight and comfortable feel.

The Razr's hinge mechanism is a key area where Motorola has excelled. Designed to withstand thousands of folds, the hinge is engineered for long-term durability and smooth operation. Unlike some competitors that may exhibit creases or stiffness over time, the Razr's hinge ensures a seamless and reliable folding experience.

The pOLED display used in the Razr is another testament to Motorola's focus on quality. This advanced display technology delivers vibrant colors, deep blacks, and sharp details while being flexible enough to support the foldable design. Additionally, Motorola has implemented protective measures, such as water-repellent coatings, to enhance the device's resilience against accidental spills or splashes.

Motorola's attention to detail extends to the external display, which is protected by Corning Gorilla Glass for added durability. This ensures that the cover screen remains scratch-resistant and can handle daily wear and tear.

Overall, the Razr's build quality reflects Motorola's dedication to creating a device that not only looks and feels premium but also performs reliably under real-world conditions.

Why the Razr 2024 Flip is a Game-Changer

The Motorola Razr 2024 Flip is a game-changer in the foldable smartphone market because it redefines what a foldable phone can be. It strikes the perfect balance between functionality, design, and innovation, offering features that cater to a wide range of users, from tech enthusiasts to fashion-conscious individuals.

One of the key reasons the Razr is a game-changer is its focus on usability. The large, functional external display allows users to accomplish more without constantly opening the phone, making it a practical choice for multitasking and on-the-go productivity. This emphasis on convenience sets the Razr apart from other foldable phones that treat the external display as an afterthought.

The Razr's ability to blend nostalgia with modern technology also makes it a standout device. Its design pays homage to the iconic flip phones of the early 2000s while incorporating state-of-the-art features like advanced cameras, 5G connectivity, and powerful performance. This unique combination appeals to users who want a device that is both innovative and familiar.

Motorola's commitment to creating a cohesive ecosystem, as seen with the Ready For platform, further enhances the Razr's appeal. By allowing the phone to function as a desktop computer, gaming console, or media hub, Motorola has expanded the possibilities of what a smartphone can do.

Finally, the Razr's emphasis on user experience, from its intuitive gestures to its durable build quality, makes it a device that is not only innovative but also practical and reliable. It is a phone that adapts to the user's needs, offering a level of versatility and convenience that few competitors can match.

The Motorola Razr 2024 Flip redefines the foldable phone experience, standing out as a unique and innovative device in a competitive market. From its advanced features and nostalgic design to its exceptional build quality and user-focused ecosystem, the Razr offers a compelling alternative to traditional smartphones and foldable competitors alike.

Using the Razr for Fitness and Wellness

T he Motorola Razr 2024 Flip isn't just a stylish and innovative smartphone; it's also a powerful companion for maintaining a healthy and balanced lifestyle. With its advanced features, compatibility with fitness apps, and seamless integration with health-tracking tools, the Razr is well-suited to support your fitness and wellness goals. Whether you're exploring fitness apps, engaging in virtual workouts, tracking your health metrics, or streaming yoga and meditation sessions, the Razr provides all the tools you need to prioritize your well-being.

Best Fitness Apps for Your Device

The Motorola Razr 2024 Flip supports a wide variety of fitness apps designed to help you stay active and monitor your progress. These apps cater to different fitness levels and preferences, providing everything from guided workouts to nutrition tracking.

Google Fit is an excellent starting point for Razr users. Pre-installed on many Android devices, Google Fit tracks your daily activities, including steps, distance, and calories burned. It integrates with a variety of wearables and other fitness apps, making it a comprehensive platform for monitoring your fitness journey.

For more specific workout guidance, apps like **Nike Training Club** and **FitOn** offer a wide range of exercises tailored to your goals. These apps provide video tutorials, customizable workout plans, and expert tips, making them ideal for home workouts or gym sessions.

If you enjoy running or cycling, **Strava** is a must-have. This app tracks your routes, distance, speed, and elevation while allowing you to compete with friends and join fitness challenges. For strength training enthusiasts, **JEFIT** provides detailed workout plans, a progress tracker, and a library of exercises to help you build muscle effectively.

To complement your physical activity, nutrition apps like **MyFitnessPal** or **Lifesum** allow you to track your meals, monitor your calorie intake, and ensure that your diet aligns with your fitness goals. These apps sync seamlessly with the Razr, providing a well-rounded approach to health and wellness.

Using the Razr for Virtual Workouts

Virtual workouts have become increasingly popular, and the Motorola Razr 2024 Flip makes it easy to join online fitness classes or follow guided sessions from the comfort of your home. With its foldable design and advanced display technology, the Razr is ideal for streaming workout videos and participating in live sessions.

The **Flex View Mode** is particularly useful for virtual workouts. By folding the phone partially and placing it on a flat surface, you can create a built-in stand that allows you to follow workout instructions hands-free. This setup is perfect for yoga, Pilates, or high-intensity interval training (HIIT) sessions, as it keeps the screen at an optimal viewing angle without the need for additional accessories.

For live workout sessions, apps like **Peloton**, **Obé Fitness**, and **Alo Moves** offer real-time classes led by professional instructors. These apps provide a wide range of classes, from strength training and cardio to dance and barre. You can connect to these sessions easily using the Razr's high-resolution screen and fast 5G connectivity, ensuring smooth streaming without interruptions.

If you prefer guided workouts at your own pace, platforms like **YouTube** and **Beachbody On Demand** offer pre-recorded fitness videos covering a variety of exercises. The Razr's dual speakers and vibrant display enhance the experience, making each session engaging and motivating.

Health Tracking and Integration

The Motorola Razr 2024 Flip integrates seamlessly with health-tracking devices and apps, allowing you to monitor your overall well-being effectively. The phone supports popular fitness wearables like Fitbit, Garmin, and Samsung Galaxy Watch, which can sync data directly to apps on your Razr.

Health tracking apps such as **Google Fit** and **Samsung Health** provide a centralized platform for monitoring your fitness data. These apps can track metrics like heart rate, sleep patterns, stress levels, and activity levels, giving you a comprehensive overview of your health. You can also set goals, receive personalized insights, and get reminders to stay active throughout the day.

For those who value mental wellness, apps like **Headspace** and **Calm** offer mindfulness exercises, stress-reducing activities, and sleep tracking features. These apps sync effortlessly with your device, allowing you to incorporate mental health practices into your daily routine.

The Razr also supports **NFC (Near Field Communication)**, enabling you to connect with gym equipment or health monitoring devices that support this technology. For example, some smart treadmills and stationary bikes can sync your workout data to your phone, giving you a detailed summary of your performance.

Streaming Yoga and Meditation Sessions

Yoga and meditation are excellent practices for improving flexibility, reducing stress, and enhancing overall well-being. The Motorola Razr 2024 Flip is an ideal tool for accessing high-quality yoga and meditation content, whether through apps, streaming services, or live sessions.

Apps like **Yoga for Beginners, Glo,** and **Down Dog** provide guided yoga classes for users of all skill levels. These apps allow you to choose the duration, intensity, and focus of your practice, making it easy to fit yoga into your schedule. The Razr's foldable design allows you to prop the phone up in Flex View Mode, creating a hands-free setup that's perfect for following poses and sequences.

For meditation, apps like **Calm, Insight Timer,** and **Smiling Mind** offer a variety of guided sessions focusing on mindfulness, relaxation, and stress reduction. These apps are great for morning meditations to start your day or evening practices to unwind before bed.

Streaming platforms like **YouTube** also host a wealth of yoga and meditation content, from beginner tutorials to advanced practices. The Razr's dual speakers provide clear audio for guided sessions, while the vibrant display ensures that visuals like poses and breathing techniques are easy to follow.

If you prefer live sessions, platforms like **Zoom** or **Alo Moves** allow you to join virtual classes led by professional instructors. The Razr's high-quality camera and microphone make it easy to interact with instructors and fellow participants, creating an immersive experience.

The Motorola Razr 2024 Flip is a versatile and powerful companion for fitness and wellness. Whether you're exploring fitness apps, joining virtual workouts, tracking your health metrics, or streaming yoga and meditation sessions, the Razr offers a range of features that make it easy to prioritize your well-being. Its innovative design, seamless app integration, and high-quality display create an engaging and motivating environment for achieving your health goals.

Understanding Your Warranty and Support

The Motorola Razr 2024 Flip is a premium device built to deliver an exceptional user experience, but even high-quality technology can encounter issues. Understanding your warranty and support options is crucial for ensuring that your device is well-protected and that you can resolve any problems efficiently. This chapter explores what the warranty covers, how to get repairs for your Razr, the process of contacting Motorola support, and ways to extend your warranty for added peace of mind.

What the Warranty Covers

Motorola offers a standard warranty with every Razr 2024 Flip purchase, covering manufacturing defects and hardware issues that arise due to faulty materials or workmanship. This warranty typically lasts for one year from the date of purchase, although the duration may vary depending on your region or retailer.

The warranty covers issues such as problems with the foldable display, hinge mechanism, internal components, or battery malfunctions that are not caused by user damage. For instance, if the hinge becomes stiff or the screen develops unresponsive areas due to manufacturing defects, these issues would fall under warranty coverage.

However, it's essential to understand what the warranty does not cover. Damages caused by accidents, misuse, unauthorized repairs, or exposure to water beyond the phone's resistance rating are excluded. For example, if the device is dropped and the screen cracks, this would not be covered under the standard warranty. Additionally, cosmetic damage, such as scratches or wear and tear, is also excluded.

To ensure your warranty remains valid, avoid tampering with the device, such as attempting unauthorized repairs or modifications. Always keep your purchase receipt and warranty documentation, as these will be required to verify your eligibility for warranty claims.

Getting Repairs for Your Razr

If your Motorola Razr 2024 Flip requires repairs, it's essential to follow the correct process to ensure the issue is resolved effectively and your warranty remains intact. Motorola provides authorized service centers that are equipped to handle repairs using genuine parts, ensuring the quality and integrity of your device.

To initiate a repair, start by contacting Motorola support to diagnose the issue. In some cases, the support team may provide troubleshooting steps that can resolve the problem without requiring a repair. If the issue persists and a repair is needed, you will be directed to the nearest authorized service center.

When visiting a service center, bring your device, purchase receipt, and warranty documentation. The technicians will assess the issue and determine if it is covered under the warranty. If the problem falls outside of warranty coverage, such as accidental damage, you will receive a cost estimate for the repair before proceeding.

For minor issues, repairs may be completed on the same day. However, more complex problems may require the device to be sent to a specialized repair facility, which can take several days. Motorola's repair services prioritize using original parts to maintain the performance and durability of your Razr.

In regions where authorized service centers are not available, Motorola may offer mail-in repair services. This involves shipping your device to a repair facility, where it will be serviced and returned to you. Always use Motorola's official channels for repairs to avoid voiding your warranty.

Contacting Motorola Support

Motorola's customer support team is available to assist with a wide range of issues, from troubleshooting and warranty claims to general inquiries about your Razr 2024 Flip. Contacting support is straightforward, with multiple options available to suit your preferences.

The easiest way to reach Motorola support is through their website, where you can access a comprehensive help center. This platform includes FAQs, troubleshooting guides, and step-by-step instructions for resolving common issues. If you require further assistance, you can initiate a live chat with a support agent directly from the website.

For more personalized support, you can contact Motorola's customer service via phone. The phone number for your region can be found on the Motorola website. When calling, have your device information, such as the IMEI number and purchase details, ready to streamline the process.

Motorola also offers a support app that can be downloaded onto your Razr. This app provides diagnostic tools, warranty information, and a direct line to customer support, making it a convenient option for addressing issues on the go.

If you prefer social media, Motorola's official accounts on platforms like Twitter and Facebook often respond to customer inquiries. This can be a quick way to get help for basic questions or concerns. Regardless of the method you choose, Motorola's support team is trained to provide clear and helpful solutions.

For added peace of mind, Motorola offers extended warranty plans that provide coverage beyond the standard warranty period. These plans, often referred to as **Motorola Care** or **Moto Care**, are designed to protect your investment and reduce the cost of repairs in the long term.

An extended warranty typically includes coverage for accidental damage, such as drops, spills, or screen cracks. This is especially valuable for a foldable device like the Razr, as repairs for foldable displays and hinge mechanisms can be costly without coverage.

To purchase an extended warranty, visit Motorola's website or contact their support team. You can usually enroll in a plan within a specific timeframe after purchasing your device, such as 30 or 60 days. Plans may vary in duration, with options for one, two, or even three years of additional coverage.

Some extended warranties also include perks like expedited repairs, priority customer support, and free shipping for mail-in repairs. Before purchasing a plan, carefully review the terms and conditions to understand what is covered and any exclusions that may apply.

Investing in an extended warranty is a smart choice for users who want to protect their device from unforeseen accidents or long-term wear and tear. It provides financial security and ensures that your Razr 2024 Flip remains in excellent condition throughout its lifespan.

Understanding your warranty and support options is essential for maximizing the value of your Motorola Razr 2024 Flip. By knowing what the warranty covers, following the proper steps for repairs, and exploring extended warranty plans, you can ensure that your device stays protected and performs at its best. With Motorola's comprehensive support network, you'll have access to the resources and assistance you need, giving you confidence and peace of mind as you enjoy your Razr.

Looking Ahead – Future Proofing Your Razr

The Motorola Razr 2024 Flip is a groundbreaking device that combines advanced technology with a sleek, foldable design. While it excels in its current form, it's essential to consider how you can future-proof your Razr to ensure it remains relevant and valuable as technology evolves. This chapter explores how to stay updated with Android advancements, prepare for future innovations in foldable technology, maximize your device's resale value, and understand Motorola's broader vision for the future of mobile technology.

Keeping Up with Android Updates

Keeping your Motorola Razr 2024 Flip up to date with the latest Android updates is one of the most effective ways to future-proof your device. Android updates bring new features, enhanced security, and performance improvements that ensure your phone stays compatible with emerging apps and services.

Motorola typically provides software updates for its devices, including major Android version upgrades and monthly security patches. To ensure you don't miss these updates, enable automatic updates in your settings. You can do this by navigating to **Settings > System > Software Updates** and toggling the option for automatic downloads.

Updates not only improve functionality but also protect your device from security vulnerabilities. As new threats emerge, Motorola and Google work together to release patches that safeguard your data and personal information. Staying current with these updates is essential for maintaining a secure device.

Beyond security, major Android updates often introduce innovative features like new multitasking tools, improved app integration, and enhanced AI capabilities. For instance, upcoming updates might include better optimization for foldable devices, providing new ways to utilize the Razr's unique design. Regular updates ensure your phone remains capable of handling the latest software advancements, keeping it functional and efficient.

Preparing for Foldable Innovations

Foldable smartphones like the Razr represent the future of mobile technology, with continuous innovations shaping how these devices are used. Preparing for these advancements means understanding how to adapt your usage and expectations to align with future trends.

One significant area of innovation is the foldable display. Manufacturers are working to make foldable screens more durable, flexible, and resistant to damage. While the Razr 2024 Flip already incorporates robust materials, future updates in screen technology may introduce self-healing surfaces, improved scratch resistance, and even lighter designs. Staying informed about these developments can help you decide when to upgrade or invest in new accessories that complement emerging features.

Battery technology is another area where foldables are expected to improve. Advancements in battery efficiency and capacity will ensure that foldable devices last longer on a single charge, making them even more practical for daily use. To prepare for these innovations, adopt good charging habits now, such as avoiding overcharging or exposing your device to extreme temperatures, to maintain your Razr's battery health.

Motorola's Ready For platform is also likely to evolve, expanding the Razr's compatibility with external devices and peripherals. Future versions may support more seamless integration with smart home systems, AR (augmented reality) devices, and other emerging technologies. By staying aware of these advancements, you can maximize the potential of your Razr as new features become available.

Maximizing Resale Value

Maximizing the resale value of your Motorola Razr 2024 Flip is a smart way to future-proof your investment. By maintaining your device's condition and keeping it up to date, you can ensure it retains its value over time, making it easier to upgrade to future models.

Start by protecting your Razr from physical damage. Invest in a high-quality case and screen protector specifically designed for foldable phones. These accessories safeguard the hinge and display, two of the most delicate components of the device. Additionally, store your phone in a safe place when not in use to avoid accidental drops or spills.

Regular maintenance is also crucial for preserving resale value. Clean the hinge area and external surfaces with a soft, lint-free cloth to prevent dust and debris from accumulating. Ensure that all software updates are installed to keep the device running smoothly, as potential buyers will appreciate a phone that is fully functional and up to date.

When it comes time to sell, having the original accessories and packaging can significantly increase your phone's resale value. Keep the box, charger, and user manual in good condition. If you've purchased an extended warranty, transfer it to the new owner, as this adds value and peace of mind.

Finally, use online platforms or trade-in programs to find the best resale opportunities. Websites like eBay or Swappa allow you to list your device, while Motorola's trade-in program provides a simple way to exchange your current phone for credit toward a new one. Keeping your device in excellent condition ensures you get the best possible return on your investment.

Motorola's Vision for the Future

Motorola has a clear vision for the future, focusing on innovation, sustainability, and user-centered design. Understanding this vision provides insight into how the Razr and other Motorola devices will evolve to meet the needs of a dynamic tech landscape.

One of Motorola's key priorities is advancing foldable technology. The Razr 2024 Flip is a testament to this commitment, showcasing how foldable designs can blend nostalgia with modern functionality. Moving forward, Motorola is likely to refine this concept further, introducing foldables with even thinner profiles, larger displays, and enhanced durability.

Motorola is also deeply invested in sustainability. As part of its broader corporate strategy, the company is exploring eco-friendly materials and manufacturing processes to reduce its environmental impact. Future Razr models may incorporate recyclable components, biodegradable packaging, and energy-efficient designs, aligning with the growing demand for sustainable technology.

Another area of focus is connectivity. With the rise of 5G and emerging technologies like 6G, Motorola aims to create devices that leverage these advancements for faster speeds, lower latency, and more seamless integration with the Internet of Things (IoT). This vision ensures that Motorola devices remain at the forefront of connectivity, empowering users to stay connected in increasingly sophisticated ways.

Motorola is also enhancing its ecosystem through platforms like Ready For, which enable cross-device functionality and expand the Razr's capabilities. Future updates may include more seamless integration with wearables, smart home devices, and augmented reality tools, further blurring the lines between smartphones and other tech devices.

Looking ahead, the Motorola Razr 2024 Flip is well-positioned to adapt to the evolving landscape of mobile technology. By staying updated with Android advancements, preparing for foldable innovations, maintaining your device's value, and embracing Motorola's forward-thinking vision, you can ensure that your Razr remains a reliable and relevant part of your digital life.